# FORAGING
# FLORIDA

# HELP US KEEP THIS GUIDE UP TO DATE

Every effort has been made by the author and editors to make this guide as accurate and useful as possible. However, many things can change after a guide is published—regulations change, facilities come under new management, and so forth.

We would love to hear from you concerning your experiences with this guide and how you feel it could be improved and kept up to date. While we may not be able to respond to all comments and suggestions, we'll take them to heart, and we'll also make certain to share them with the author. Please send your comments and suggestions to falconeditorial@rowman.com.

**Thanks for your input!**

# FORAGING FLORIDA

Finding, Identifying, and Preparing Edible
and Medicinal Wild Foods in Florida

## Roger L. Hammer

FALCON GUIDES

ESSEX. CONNECTICUT

# FALCONGUIDES®

An imprint of Globe Pequot, the trade division of The Rowman & Littlefield Publishing Group, Inc.
4501 Forbes Blvd., Ste. 200
Lanham, MD 20706
www.rowman.com

Falcon and FalconGuides are registered trademarks and Make Adventure Your Story is a trademark of The Rowman & Littlefield Publishing Group, Inc.

Distributed by NATIONAL BOOK NETWORK

Photos by Roger L. Hammer unless noted otherwise.
Maps by The Rowman & Littlefield Publishing Group, Inc.

British Library Cataloguing in Publication Information available

**Library of Congress Cataloging-in-Publication Data**

Names: Hammer, Roger L., author.
Title: Foraging Florida : finding, identifying, and preparing edible and
   medicinal wild foods in Florida / Roger L. Hammer.
Description: Essex, Connecticut : FalconGuides, [2023] | Includes
   bibliographical references and index. | Summary: "Florida naturalist
   Roger Hammer highlights edible and medicinal native and naturalized
   plants found throughout the state, from the far western Panhandle to the
   island chain of the Florida Keys. The book is organized by plant family
   so foragers can learn which species are closely related, and it includes
   a poisonous plant section so novices will know which plants to avoid.
   Also features recipes, identification tips, and how to prepare herbal
   and medicinal teas"— Provided by publisher.
Identifiers: LCCN 2023002911 (print) | LCCN 2023002912 (ebook) | ISBN
   9781493069798 (paperback) | ISBN 9781493069804 (epub)
Subjects: LCSH: Wild plants, Edible—Florida—Identification. | Medicinal
   plants—Florida—Identification. | Edible
   mushrooms—Florida—Identification.
Classification: LCC QK98.5.U6 H36 2023 (print) | LCC QK98.5.U6 (ebook) |
   DDC 581.6/3209759—dc23/eng/20230421
LC record available at https://lccn.loc.gov/2023002911
LC ebook record available at https://lccn.loc.gov/2023002912

♾️™ The paper used in this publication meets the minimum requirements of American National Standard for Information Sciences—Permanence of Paper for Printed Library Materials, ANSI/NISO Z39.48-1992.

*My love affair with nature is so deep that I am not satisfied with being a mere onlooker, or nature tourist. I crave a more real and meaningful relationship. The spicy teas and tasty delicacies I prepare from wild ingredients are the bread and wine in which I have communion and fellowship with nature, and with the Author of that nature.*

—Euell Gibbons

# CONTENTS

ALABAMA

GEORGIA

Pensacola

Tallahassee

Jacksonville

ATLANTIC
OCEAN

Gainesville

Daytona Beach

Orlando

Tampa

St. Petersburg

FLORIDA

GULF OF MEXICO

Fort Lauderdale

Naples

Miami

N

0                                    100 Miles
0                  100KM

Key West

# ACKNOWLEDGMENTS

First and foremost, heartfelt love and endearment go to my lovely young wife, Michelle. She enjoys being outdoors in wild Florida, and if I could choose anyone to be with while hiking in Florida's wilds, I would choose to be with her. Also, my deepest gratitude goes to everyone who has been gracious enough to spend time with me in the field over many decades. Those who have passed away but still linger in my memories are Loran Anderson, Dan Austin, George Avery, Rob Campbell, Donovan and Helen Correll, Marjory Stoneman Douglas, Don and Joyce Gann, Hal Horwitz, Don Keller, Bob Kelley, Jim King, Carlyle Luer, Chuck McCartney, Julia Morton, John Ogden, and Richard Workman. The best thing about memories is that they keep friends with you each and every day, unseen, unheard, but always there in spirit.

Special appreciation goes to my friends Stan Matthews of Plant Creations Nursery, John Lawson of Silent Native Nursery, and Richard and Melissa Moyroud of Mesozoic Landscapes for making it easy to photograph native species on their property. It almost felt like cheating.

I am also indebted to my many gardening and botanist friends who kept me informed of the locations of plants to photograph, or made it easier by mailing me samples of fruiting plants. Those kind souls include Bill and Marcia Boothe, Keith Bradley, Brenda Brooks, Virginia Craig, Kris DeLaney, Frida Dell'Oliver, Jim Drake, Christina Dupuy, Alan Franck, Liz Golden, Floyd Griffith, Bobby Hattaway, Craig Huegel, Eric King, Susan Kolterman, Ronald Lance, Carol Lippincott, Julie Motkowicz, Tony Pernas, Patty Phares, Marlene Rodak, Jimi Sadle, Karl Werner, Wally Wilder, Leigh Williams, and Steve Woodmansee. A special thanks also goes to my longtime archaeologist friend, Bob Carr, for his input on the early people of Florida, who were the state's first foragers. And much gratitude goes to my dear friends Marc and Maria Minno up in Gainesville, who were especially helpful in sharing their personal experiences eating wild foods, brewing herbal and medicinal teas from local plants, and then graciously mailing me samples of northern Florida plants to photograph. And a hearty thank you goes to Bryon White at Yaupon Brothers American Tea Company in Edgewater for his insight in brewing the perfect glass of yaupon tea.

Assistance with recent botanical nomenclature revisions was graciously offered by my friends Keith Bradley, Edwin Bridges, Alan Franck, Alan Weakley, and Richard Wunderlin.

I also cannot forget the long list of Facebook friends who notified me of the locations of fruiting plants all across Florida, which helped add a lot of miles to the odometer in my truck.

Finally, to our two happy rescued puppies, Layla and Satine, who were always at the gate waiting to lick me on my face in a happy tail-wagging frenzy each time I returned home.

If I left anyone out, it's because I figured they'd want a free book.

# INTRODUCTION

Florida's human history dates back at least 14,000 years to the Paleo-Indians, who were present when sea levels were much lower and when now-extinct animals roamed across the landscape. In today's world, it is difficult to envision mammoths, mastodons, saber-tooth cats, American lions, large-horned bison, dire wolves, giant sloths, and even California condors residing in Florida. Paleo-Indians, and later the Archaic Indians, were hunter-fisher-gatherers, living on the bounty of plants, animals, and aquatic life that the land and water had to offer. Archaeological evidence indicates their diet was mostly small mammals, birds, reptiles, amphibians, fruits, nuts, tubers, fish, and shellfish, all of which were abundant. Centuries later as cultures changed, their itinerant way of life was abandoned, and villages with thatched huts began to appear near abundant food sources, especially where freshwater rivers met the sea. Still later they began cultivating local plants near their settlements and became the first farmers.

Knowledge about edible and medicinal wild plants was passed on from generation to generation, and, through much trial and error, they learned about poisonous plants; gained knowledge about the medicinal properties of the local flora; became familiar with the best fiber-producing plants to make nets, rope, and clothing; experimented with making dyes for clothing and body art; and learned which woods made the best spears, bows, arrows, shelters, and dug-out canoes. They formed complex societies over the centuries and developed trade routes with other cultural groups to the north, in what is now Georgia and Alabama. The Calusa even developed trade routes from southern Florida to Cuba, making the perilous ocean voyage in canoe-like vessels carved from cypress trunks. Through writings from European explorers as early as 1513, plus archaeological excavations, the rich history of their cultures became known. And it was Spanish explorer Juan Ponce de Leon who dubbed this new land "La Pascua de la Florida" because he landed here on April 7 during Pascua Florida, the Spanish Easter.

Florida fell under Spanish rule during the time when about 350,000 native people lived here in tribes known as the Ais, Apalachee, Calusa, Choctaw, Creek, Jaega, Mayaimi, Miccosukee, Tequesta, and Timucua, among others. It was the Tequesta that Juan Ponce de Leon first encountered in 1513 in southeastern Florida, and it was the more-hostile Calusa who mortally wounded him during his expedition to southwestern Florida in 1521. He died in Cuba and was laid to rest in Puerto Rico. British explorers arrived later, and by 1763 the last of the Calusa and Tequesta in Florida relocated to Cuba as Florida fell under British control.

Later came the Seminole and Miccosukee, who broke away from the Creek of present-day Georgia and Alabama, retreating into Florida during the long Seminole Wars as they fought invading British militia and settlers. They, too, had to live off the land, and small groups of them fled into the vast and unexplored Everglades in southern Florida, where some of the last battles took place in what is now Everglades National Park.

As the wars ended and white settlers built more towns, one important industry came into being in South Florida—coontie flour—known locally as "Florida arrowroot." It is not known when the first people came to understand how to process the root of the very toxic cycad called coontie (*Zamia integrifolia*) into something edible, but it is certain that many people died in the process. Early maps of the Everglades had Long Pine Key labeled the "Koontee Hunting Grounds," where this native cycad was harvested commercially for its large root that was crushed and flushed with water to remove the toxin cycasin, then processed into a type of flour. If you ever ate the original Keebler Animal Crackers, then you have eaten coontie flour.

Other important groups of people who figured prominently in the knowledge of bush medicine and edible wild plants in America came from various tribes in Africa during the slave trade era. Some escaped slavery in Florida and joined the Seminole in the fight against white settlers, and were known as the Black Seminoles. Present-day residents in the Bahamas, Haiti, Jamaica, and other islands of the West Indies have African heritage due to the slave trade and are extremely knowledgeable about bush medicines and foraging.

Over centuries, trial and error dictated what was edible and what was toxic, but in today's Florida, this is far better understood. However, the reader should understand that what is deemed to be edible may not be all that eatable because some plant parts simply may not taste all that great unless you've been lost in the woods for a considerable length of time. So, my word of advice is to forage with due caution, and always leave plenty behind for wild creatures that depend on wild foods for their survival or the survival and health of their young.

## Scope of This Book

This book covers an assortment of native and naturalized trees, shrubs, vines, palms, herbaceous wildflowers, grasses, and sedges in Florida. Naturalized species are introduced, non-native plants that have escaped cultivation and can be found growing and reproducing in both natural habitats and disturbed sites in Florida. Non-native, naturalized plants imported from tropical regions of the world are far more prevalent in South Florida than in the rest of the state. Native and naturalized plants featured in this guide have fruits that can be picked and eaten or used to prepare side dishes, salads, pies, puddings, soups, jams, and jellies, or to make wine and cordials. Also, many plants in this guide can be used to brew nutritional and medicinal herbal teas, or have the potential to help heal wounds, relieve pain from toothache, soothe a sore throat, alleviate symptoms from colds and fevers, treat diarrhea, make eye washes, and even repel mosquitoes.

Here again, however, caution is warranted because much of what we know about medicinal wild plants is often referred to as "folk medicine" or "bush medicine," and may not be deemed safe or even effective by modern-day medical doctors.

The flora of Florida is very diverse due to varied habitats that range from flooded freshwater wetlands to nearly desert-like scrub and sandhills, and from shady hardwood forests to sunny pinelands, prairies, and beach dunes. Mangroves and other coastal species are exceptionally hardy because they must be tolerant of salty soils or even being inundated by seawater, and they must bear the brunt of storm surges created by tropical storms and hurricanes.

Although Florida lies wholly within the temperate zone, the native trees that make up the hammocks of the Florida Keys are almost purely tropical species, arriving here through natural range expansion from the Bahamas, Greater Antilles, and Mexico's Yucatan Peninsula via seeds transported in the bellies of migratory birds. Other methods of natural range expansion from the tropics to southern Florida are wind dispersal of seeds and spores (some as far away as Africa) and favorable ocean currents that disperse seeds and propagules of coastal species over long distances. Many of these native tropical species do not range north of Lake Okeechobee, and some don't range north of the Florida Keys, so South Florida offers a much more diverse flora for foragers than the rest of the state. Conversely, there are numerous species that range southward from cold temperate regions that do not occur further south than the northernmost counties in Florida. So no matter where you live in the Sunshine State, there is something worth seeking out to satisfy your hunger and perhaps even cure your ills.

## Organization

This guide is arranged alphabetically by plant family, followed by the genus and species. This will aid the reader in understanding which plants are closely related to one another. Many people are surprised to learn that the edible cashew and pistachio are in the same family as poison ivy, poison sumac, and poisonwood. So don't think that all plants in the same plant family are safe to eat—celery, parsley, coriander, anise, Queen Anne's lace, and carrots are closely related to the deadly water hemlock (*Cicuta maculata*), and garden tomatoes are close kin to deadly nightshade (*Atropa belladonna*).

Common names offered in this guide include those that are most frequently used in Florida and are generally those found on the online Florida Plant Atlas, but if you are not well versed in the flora of Florida, ***never ever*** rely solely on common names as a means of identifying plants. Common names can change from region to region throughout a plant's natural range, or they can change from one language to another. The message here is to always err on the side of caution if you are even the slightest bit uncertain of a plant's identity. It could save you a trip to the hospital, or worse.

## Outdoor Ethics and Legalities

Be aware that harvesting fruits, seeds, or other plant parts on public lands may be illegal. Public lands include national, state, and county parks and preserves, national and state forests, Water Management District properties, and state wildlife management areas, so be sure to check before foraging or risk being fined. Some national parks outside Florida, especially in the American West, allow harvesting limited quantities of fruits for personal consumption, such as wild blueberries and blackberries, but foraging is not allowed in Everglades National Park or in any of Florida's state parks. Fishing is allowed in Everglades National Park as well as in Florida state parks, so not being allowed to sample a blueberry or a cocoplum makes no logical sense, but rules are rules until they are changed.

However, non-commercial harvesting of fruits for personal consumption in designated wildlife management areas, including state and national forests and preserves, is legal with a day-use permit. These include Big Cypress National Preserve, Apalachicola National Forest, Ocala National Forest, Osceola National Forest, Goethe State Forest, Tate's Hell, and others. To acquire a permit for foraging in Florida's national forests, go to https://apps.fs.usda.gov/gp.

Private landowners may allow foraging on large ranches or other lands, but check with the owners to avoid trespassing charges. In areas where you are allowed to forage, a good rule of thumb is to avoid overharvesting and leave plenty behind for local wildlife. A better option, and one that I wholeheartedly encourage, is to cultivate the plants you wish to harvest from and have them available right at your doorstep.

Also be aware that some native plants are federal- or state-listed endangered or threatened species, so it is illegal to harvest any parts of them without a permit from the Florida Department of Agriculture and Consumer Services Division of Plant Industry obtained fourteen days prior to harvesting. If endangered or threatened plants are on private property, then you must have the property owner's permission in writing. However, many threatened and endangered species are available from nurseries that specialize in Florida native plants so it is perfectly legal for you to grow them as a food source.

As mentioned previously, some plants in this guide are not native to Florida but have escaped cultivation and can be found growing wild in native habitats. Some of these non-native plants may be listed as Category I or Category II invasive species by the Florida Invasive Species Council because they invade and adversely impact native habitats. Some examples of Category I invasive species in

Florida with edible fruits are guava (*Psidium guajava*), Surinam cherry (*Eugenia uniflora*), and sapodilla (*Manilkara zapota*). You may even find pecans, tomatoes, citrus, loquats, mangoes, canistel, melons, and avocados growing wild in parts of Florida. If you consume the fruits of these species in the wild, carry the seeds out with you and dispose of them so you do not contribute to their spread. An equally important message is, if you bring fruits from home when you go on hiking or camping trips, do not discard the seeds because that is exactly how many non-native plants become established.

## Disclaimer

It stands to reason that anyone using this or other books on edible and medicinal wild plants should use due caution when eating wild foods, and especially plants used in bush medicine or folk medicine, because many of the medicinal plants mentioned in this guide have not been tested and approved by medical research even though they have been used by indigenous people for centuries. The uses of the plants included in this guide are found in the modern literature, or from personal experience, but in no way are they all deemed to be safe for everyone, so before you decide to try self-medication, consult a physician, ethnobotanist, or herbalist. Some plants, such as persimmon, seagrape, hogplum, Chickasaw plum, cocoplum, walnuts, blueberries, blackberries, and purslane, are well-known edibles throughout their natural range in Florida, while many others may be foreign to foragers new to Florida. And it cannot be emphasized enough that proper identification is paramount no matter where you are foraging.

## Grow Your Own

I encourage you to consider growing your own wild foods as an option to harvesting from the wild. This benefits native wildlife that depend on wild foods for their survival, and especially for birds to feed their young during nesting season. Many Florida native plants can now be found in specialty nurseries throughout the state, so by using native plants in your landscape, you have a readily available source not only to harvest and enjoy, but also to create a habitat on your own property to attract birds, butterflies, and other wildlife to share the bounty. With development threatening wild habitats throughout Florida, creating wildlife corridors in urban areas will be critical for wildlife. It's a win-win. For a listing of nurseries in Florida that specialize in native plants, visit the Florida Association of Native Nurseries website at www.fann.org.

Perhaps it goes without saying, but be absolutely certain that your children know to never eat any plant parts without adult supervision. There are many common native and non-native plants, both wild and cultivated in Florida, that are toxic, and some have caused deaths of children (and pets) in Florida. See the Poisonous Plants chapter in this guide.

## Join the Florida Native Plant Society

Florida Native Plant Society state conferences offer native plant sales from local vendors, and chapter meetings often host plant raffles and sales. To become a member, visit the Florida Native Plant Society website at www.fnps.org. Once you are a member, attend the chapter meetings near you and enjoy the camaraderie. Not only do chapters have guest speakers each month, they often offer guided field trips to local preserves with leaders who can identify plants in their natural habitats, which is a great way to learn, especially if you are new to Florida.

## Florida Habitats

### Upland Deciduous Hardwood Forests, Bottomland Forests, and River Forests

These temperate forests are composed of evergreen and deciduous hardwoods or a mix of hardwoods and cypress. They may be dry (xeric), moist (mesic), or even flooded (hydric), so the plant species that make up these forests are extremely diverse. Some of Florida's prettiest rivers flow through these forests, including the fabled Suwannee River.

### Pine Flatwoods and High Pine

Pine flatwoods are floristically rich, sparsely stocked with pines (*Pinus* spp.) and patches of saw palmetto (*Serenoa repens*). Fire plays an important role in maintaining pine flatwoods, so to see a riot of wildflowers, check this plant community within a few weeks or months following fire. Look also for saucer-shaped-depression marshes within this habitat for an entirely different pallet of wildflowers, including carnivorous species like pitcher-plants, bladderworts, sundews, and butterworts. High pine habitat is dry, with an overstory of pines and an understory dominated by grasses.

### Pine Rocklands

Pine rocklands occur in southern Florida, especially on the Miami Rock Ridge in southern Miami-Dade County, Long Pine Key in Everglades National Park, and Big Pine Key in the lower Florida Keys. Pine rocklands are characterized by outcroppings of bare, jagged, oolitic limestone, often with numerous solution holes that make travel by foot difficult and sometimes painful. The overstory tree is the South Florida slash pine (*Pinus densa*), with a rich understory of mostly tropical shrubs, or trees that are kept shrubby by fire, growing among grasses, sedges, herbaceous wildflowers, and palms. Saw palmetto (*Serenoa repens*) is a common understory species in pine rockland habitat on the southern Florida mainland, but is nearly absent on Big Pine Key, where it is replaced by Florida thatch palm (*Thrinax radiata*) and Key thatch palm (*Leucothrinax morrisii*). A locally common palm in the understory of pine rocklands is the Florida silver palm (*Coccothrinax argentata*).

### Tropical Hardwood Hammocks

Hammocks in southernmost Florida are dominated by hardwood trees of tropical origin. These tropical trees arrived here by seeds transported across the Straits of Florida and the Gulf of Mexico in the bellies of migratory songbirds, as well as by tropical storms and ocean currents. There is very little understory in mature tropical hammocks, and most have deep solution holes carved into the limestone that hold water during the rainy season. The walls of these solution holes offer critical habitat for a variety of ferns and liverworts.

### Mangroves

Mangrove forests are the least floristically diverse plant community in Florida, yet they are a critically important nursery ground for countless fish and marine organisms, and they provide essential roosting and nesting sites for herons, egrets, cormorants, brown pelicans, magnificent frigatebirds, and many other birds. The tree that typically dominates this plant community is the red mangrove (*Rhizophora mangle*), which produces a tangled maze of arching prop roots. Mangroves are protected because of their crucial role in buffering Florida's shorelines from hurricane winds and storm surges.

### Salt Marsh

Like mangroves, salt marshes are floristically challenged because they are inundated during parts of the year with saline water. The dominant plant in salt marshes is saltwort (*Batis maritima*), but all plants that make up this habitat must be able to tolerate extremely harsh conditions. Other species found in this habitat include sea blite (*Suaeda linearis*), annual glasswort (*Salicornia bigelovii*), perennial glasswort (*Salicornia ambigua*), and saltgrass (*Distichlis spicata*).

### Cypress Swamps and Mixed Hardwood Swamps

Cypress swamps are dominated by either bald cypress (*Taxodium distichum*) or pond cypress (*Taxodium ascendens*). Some are dome shaped, with taller trees in the deeper center, graduating to smaller trees toward the outer fringe. Cypress domes form in depressions and are commonly seen in Big Cypress National Preserve and Everglades National Park. Three of the most famous swamps in Florida are the Fakahatchee Swamp and Corkscrew Swamp in southwest Florida and the famed Okefenokee Swamp in southeastern Georgia and northeastern Florida, forming the headwaters of the Suwannee River. Swamps may be flooded all year or dry in late winter. Linear swamps are called strands and may be intermixed with cypress and broad-leaved hardwoods. Strands are basically shallow, forested rivers. Deeper drainage areas in swamps are called sloughs, where you will typically find pond apple (*Annona glabra*) and pop ash (*Fraxinus caroliniana*) trees.

## Dry Prairies

The Kissimmee Prairie encompasses tens of thousands of acres of dry prairie, and much of it is protected within Kissimmee Prairie Preserve State Park and the adjacent Avon Park Air Force Range north and west of Lake Okeechobee. Here you will find vast, open, essentially treeless grasslands interrupted by patches of saw palmetto (*Serenoa repens*) and dwarf live oak (*Quercus minima*) that are kept low and shrubby by frequent fires. Dry prairies can be flooded at times, although the duration is short due to the sandy substrate that drains quickly.

## Wet Prairies

Wet prairies are scattered throughout mainland Florida, and good examples can be seen at Paynes Prairie in northern Florida as well as Big Cypress National Preserve and Everglades National Park in southern Florida. They can be categorized as short-hydroperiod or long-hydroperiod glades, depending on how long they are flooded during the year. Short-hydroperiod glades are flooded only during the rainy season, from summer into fall. Wet prairies and dry prairies are both dependent on flooding and fire, and are rich in wildflowers.

## Beach Dunes

A prerequisite for beach dune vegetation is the ability to tolerate dry, nutrient-deficient sand along with salt spray and occasional inundation by saltwater from tides and storm surges. Beach dune plants must also be able to survive the full fury of hurricanes and storm surges. They are a hardy bunch of plants, and many species play a vital role in stabilizing beach sand from erosion by wind and tides.

## Scrub and Sandhills

These plant communities are combined because both are relict beach dunes created when sea levels were much higher than they are today. Scrub habitat on the Lake Wales Ridge, which stretches down the center of peninsular Florida from Lake County to Highlands County, has the highest percentage of endemic plant species in the state because it was once an isolated island when the Florida Plateau was submerged. Some important portions of the Lake Wales Ridge are protected within Archbold Biological Station, Lake Wales Ridge National Wildlife Refuge, and Tiger Creek Preserve. Sandhills are typically characterized by low, rolling hills sparsely populated by pines. Coastal sandhills are often referred to as scrubby flatwoods.

# Poisonous Plants

For obvious reasons, anyone interested in edible wild plants should first learn which plants are poisonous, especially those that can be fatal if consumed. While there are quite a few Florida native plants that have poisonous properties, there are also a number of poisonous plants from other parts of the world that are purposely cultivated in home gardens or have become naturalized in undisturbed native habitats, vacant lots, along roadsides, or even as weeds in home landscapes. Poisonous plants are not only those that can be fatal if ingested, but also species that can cause mild to serious health issues, such as liver damage, elevated heart rate, convulsions, vomiting, temporary blindness, or mild to severe skin rashes. Some wild plants have proven to be carcinogenic and should be avoided, or at least not consumed on a regular basis. Still others are abortifacients and should not be consumed by women in early stages of pregnancy. It should be noted that some plants may be toxic at certain stages of growth, but non-toxic in other stages, so do your homework before foraging.

Also pay deserved attention to plants that are high in oxalates, or oxalic acid. Many fruits, vegetables, and nuts found in supermarkets are high in oxalates—most notably spinach, Swiss chard, kale, rhubarb, parsley, pecans, walnuts, carambolas, and even the sweet potato. Wild plants that are high in oxalates include wood sorrel (*Oxalis*), purslane (*Portulaca*), amaranth (*Amaranthus*), and pokeweed (*Phytolacca*). Oxalates have been linked to a variety of health issues such as kidney stones, thyroid diseases, cystic fibrosis, autism, fibromyalgia (muscle pain), and chronic fatigue, so it is wise to moderate your intake of plants that are known to be high in oxalates, especially if you are prone to developing kidney stones.

Again, never rely on common names of plants for identification. For example, in Florida the name moonflower relates to a harmless morning-glory (*Ipomoea alba*) with white flowers that open at night, but the name moonflower in Texas refers to the highly toxic *Datura wrightii*.

# ANACARDIACEAE (CASHEW FAMILY)

## POISONWOOD
*Metopium toxiferum*

**Native**

A large tree in hammocks or kept shrubby in pine rocklands by fire. Compound leaves bear 3–7 (usually 5) ovate to obovate leaflets, each averaging about 3" long and 2" wide. Small, yellowish flowers are in open panicles, and female trees produce small, oblong, mustard-colored fruits. The bark on mature trees peels off in irregular strips, with black patches where the sap has been exposed to the air. The sap can cause a mild to severe blistering skin rash on sensitive people, and eating the fruits can cause lesions in the mouth, throat, and digestive tract. Also, smoke from burning poisonwood can cause extreme eye and throat irritation. Nevertheless, white-crowned pigeons and other birds savor the fruits. My favorite poisonwood tree is along the Gumbo Limbo Trail in Everglades National Park, where some hapless soul carved his and his girlfriend's initials into the trunk of the tree with a knife while toxic sap oozed out of the cuts. I often wonder if they're still together.

## POISON IVY
*Toxicodendron radicans*

**Native**

Though perhaps the most well-known poisonous plant in the United States, it is surprising how few people can correctly identify it. Poison ivy has compound leaves with 3 leaflets, which may be entire, lobed on one or both sides, with each leaflet ranging 1"–4" long. In wintertime the leaflets turn red. The trunk of the vine will root to anything it touches, such as tree trunks, buildings, or utility poles. Small, green flowers produce white, round, ⅛" fruits that birds eat. The sap can cause a mild to severe rash on sensitive people, but there are products in your local pharmacy that can be applied before you go on hikes in poison ivy territory, and other products that can be rubbed on your skin after you have come in contact with the sap. Poison ivy is found statewide, but the related poison oak (*Toxicodendron pubescens*) only occurs from the Panhandle south to Highlands County. It is more shrub-like with hairy, toothed leaflets.

## POISON SUMAC
*Toxicodendron vernix*

**Native**

Poison sumac is a shrub or small tree found from Highlands County northward up the center of the Florida peninsula and west across the Panhandle. It has compound leaves with lanceolate leaflets measuring about 1" wide and 3" long. The toxin and warnings are the same as poison ivy.

# APIACEAE (CARROT FAMILY)

## SPOTTED WATER HEMLOCK
*Cicuta maculata*

**Native**

This highly toxic and potentially deadly species is considered to be the most poisonous native plant in the United States. It ranges in Florida from Escambia County to Nassau County south to Collier and Broward Counties. It is typically found in wet areas, such as along roadside ditches, lake and pond margins, or the banks of streams, springs, and rivers. The flowers resemble the edible elderberry (*Sambucus canadensis*), so due caution is highly advised. Spotted water hemlock is a shrub with alternate, toothed, compound leaves. The small, white flowers are in saucer-size umbels, and the notch at the tip of each petal is a notable characteristic not present on elderberry flower petals. Ingestion of any part of this plant can prove fatal, so be extraordinarily cautious if you are a novice and you think you've identified elderberry or other non-toxic look-alike members of the carrot family, such as Queen Anne's lace (*Daucus carota*).

## MADAGASCAR PERIWINKLE
*Catharanthus roseus*

Introduced

This plant is well-known to Florida gardeners and is commonly sold in garden centers and nurseries throughout Florida. It escapes cultivation and can be found inhabiting beaches, sandhills, pinelands, and disturbed sites throughout much of Florida. The plant is very toxic to grazing animals, including dogs, and has caused poisoning in humans as well. Symptoms include tremors, fever, nausea, and nerve damage. Although death is unlikely, seek urgent medical attention if symptoms occur.

## OLEANDER
*Nerium oleander*

### Introduced

Although oleander is not naturalized in Florida, it is a very common landscape plant due to its colorful blossoms that are typically white, red, or pink. All parts of the plant are toxic, and a single leaf, chewed and swallowed, can cause grave poisoning and even death. Smoke from burning stems and leaves is very toxic and can cause hospitalization. It is best to not grow oleander if you have children or pets, and yet it is surprising how often it is seen as a landscape plant around elementary schools and neighborhood parks.

## MANGROVE RUBBERVINE
*Rhabdadenia biflora*

**Native**

This pretty vine occurs from Brevard and Sarasota Counties south along both coasts into the Florida Keys. It inhabits coastal habitats, including mangrove/buttonwood forests and along the fringes of salt marsh habitat. The white sap is toxic both externally and internally, with the potential of causing severe skin blisters or inflammation of the mouth, throat, and stomach.

# CUCURBITACEAE (GOURD FAMILY)

## BALSAM PEAR
*Momordica charantia*

**Introduced**

This Category II invasive species has ill-smelling, deeply lobed leaves with yellow flowers measuring about 1" wide that produce warty, gourd-like, 1½" fruits. The fruits turn orange when ripe, splitting open to reveal seeds coated with a red, edible aril. The leaves, seeds, and orange, fleshy rind are purgative if eaten. The fruits are hypoglycemic and will lower blood sugar levels if eaten; and in the West Indies and elsewhere, quantities of ripe fruits are eaten as an abortifacient, so women in early stages of pregnancy should avoid consuming any parts of this plant. Also, juice extracted from the vine has caused fatalities to children. However, the cooked leaves are considered edible and nutritious, and the green, unripe fruits are pickled in Jamaica and are known as "bitter gourds" in Oriental cooking. First and foremost, however, it should be regarded as a poisonous plant, and it should be noted that the fruits have caused fatal poisoning in dogs.

# EUPHORBIACEAE (SPURGE FAMILY)

## MANCHINEEL
*Hippomane mancinella*

**Native**
Manchineel is a small to medium-sized, spreading, deciduous tree bearing glossy, ovate leaves with scalloped margins. Short spikes of tiny yellow flowers produce oval, green fruits to about 1½" wide that may be blushed with pink on one side. It is native to South Florida and can be found in coastal forests of Miami-Dade and Monroe Counties, both mainland and the Florida Keys. All parts of the tree are toxic, and simply sitting beneath a tree in the rain can cause burning of the eyes, temporary blindness, and skin irritation. Contact with the sap causes burning and reddening of the skin accompanied by a long-lasting, festering rash. Eating the sweet-tasting fruits can cause severe gastrointestinal pain and can be fatal. In other parts of its range, it is called *arbol de la muerte* (tree of death), but there are no Florida fatalities reported in the modern literature. Still, however, it is definitely a tree to admire from a distance.

## CASTORBEAN
*Ricinus communis*

**Introduced**

Castorbean is native to the Mediterranean region, eastern Africa, and India but is widely naturalized throughout many regions of the world, including Florida. Although castorbean is sometimes cultivated as an ornamental, it is a Category II invasive species, especially in the lower half of Florida where it colonizes disturbed sites such as canal banks, overgrown lots, roadsides, and edges of woodlands that are bisected by roads. It is a non-woody species that can reach 10' tall or more, with large, green or burgundy, deeply lobed, palmate leaves. Male flowers are yellowish green with cream-colored stamens, and female flowers bear prominent red stigmas. Green to reddish fruits bear soft spines and produce shiny, beanlike, mottled seeds. Although the seeds are the source of medicinal castor oil, they also contain ricin, one of the world's deadliest toxins. Poisonings are rare, but consuming several seeds have killed children in Florida and six seeds are enough to kill a horse. Some people experience respiratory distress when standing near flowering castorbean plants. It is puzzling why this dangerous plant is grown as an ornamental.

## QUEEN'S DELIGHT
*Stillingia sylvatica*

**Native**

This species produces an irritating, milky sap as well as substances that can promote tumors, so it should not be consumed or used externally for any reason. It is found in pinelands and other sandy habitats. The similar *Stillingia aquatica*, found in wet habitats, bears the same warning.

# FABACEAE (PEA FAMILY)

## ROSARY PEA
*Abrus precatorius*

**Introduced**

Rosary pea (also called crab eyes and jequirity bean) is a vine native to the Old World tropics but naturalized in tropical and warm temperate regions world-wide. In Florida it is listed as a Category I invasive species. Leaves are finely pinnate with small, oblong leaflets. Small, pink to lavender flowers are followed by green pods that turn brown before splitting open to reveal clusters of hard, shiny, red-and-black seeds. A single seed contains enough of the toxin abrin to be fatal, and is twice as toxic as ricin, found in the seeds of castorbean. If a mature seed is swallowed whole and intact, it will pass through the body without harm, but if a single seed is cracked or chewed, it can be fatal without urgent medical attention. Immature seeds are especially dangerous to children.

## NECKLACE POD
*Sophora tomentosa* var. *truncata*

**Native**

This attractive shrub is native to Florida and has been joined in the nursery trade by var. *occidentalis*, a non-native, tropical American relative that produces silvery pubescent leaves, but otherwise they are practically identical. Both have long, terminal spikes of yellow, pealike flowers and bear pods that constrict around each seed, somewhat resembling a pearl necklace. Although the seeds are toxic, there are no reported poisonings in Florida. It is included here as a warning because it is in the Florida nursery trade and the necklace-like pods may be attractive to young children. Consuming the seeds can cause violent vomiting and purging that requires medical attention.

# GELSEMIACEAE (GELSEMIUM FAMILY)

## CAROLINA JESSAMINE
*Gelsemium sempervirens*

**Native**

All parts of this vine are poisonous, and it has caused human fatalities in Florida. It is found throughout the Florida Panhandle south through mainland Florida to Charlotte and Palm Beach Counties. It is a popular landscape plant in parts of Florida but is not a wise choice if you have young children or pets. Oddly, it is sold as a homeopathic medicine in pellet form for stress relief, but it would be prudent to consult a physician before taking it.

# IRIDACEAE (IRIS FAMILY)

## IRIS
*Iris savannarum* (pictured) and 7 other native species

The rhizomes of *Iris* species are mildly to dangerously toxic to humans if consumed, and the leaves and flowers can be fatal to cats, dogs, and livestock. Place *Iris* species on your do-not-eat list.

# MELANTHIACEAE (BUNCHFLOWER FAMILY)

## FLYPOISON
*Amianthium muscaetoxicum*

**Native**

All parts of this plant are poisonous if ingested, especially the underground bulb, and there are documented human deaths from eating the bulb, including children. A traditional use of the plant was to crush the bulb and mix it with sugar to poison flies. It is found throughout the Florida Panhandle.

## CROWPOISON OR OSCEOLA'S PLUME
*Stenanthium densum*

**Native**
All parts of this plant are toxic to humans and grazing livestock. Native Americans and early settlers mixed corn with crushed bulbs to poison crows that invaded their crops. It is often found in open prairies or in pine flatwoods, and ranges south in Florida to Lake Okeechobee. Two other species occur in the Florida Panhandle.

## SANDBOG DEATHCAMAS
*Zigadenus glaberrimus*

**Native**

All parts of this plant are toxic to people, livestock, and pets. In Florida, its natural range is restricted to the Panhandle. It should go without saying that you should not eat any plant with the word "death" in its common name.

# VERBENACEAE (VERBENA FAMILY)

## SHRUB VERBENA
*Lantana strigocamara*

### Introduced

This Category I invasive species is widely naturalized in Florida, and many culti-vars are in the Florida nursery trade. The green, unripe fruits can be fatal if eaten. The leaves can kill grazing livestock and can give dogs severe liver disorders. While some foragers eat the ripe fruits and even eat the fresh, new leaves or make a tea from the leaves, this is ill-advised due to liver toxins. In short, remove this species from your home garden, do not purchase it from nurseries, and do not consume any part of it, despite what you may read otherwise.

# ZAMIACEAE (ZAMIA FAMILY)

## COONTIE
*Zamia integrifolia*

All parts of coontie are toxic and can be fatal if eaten, especially the large, underground root and the seeds on female plants. Somehow the Seminole tribe in Florida learned how to take the large root, crush it, and then place it in a stream to wash away the water-soluble toxin called cycasin. They then ground it into flour for baking Seminole bread and biscuits. White settlers later harvested and processed the roots commercially as Florida arrowroot, which became one of the first industries in South Florida. It is a popular landscape plant and a larval host plant of the imperiled atala butterfly.

# FLORIDA NATIVE PLANTS TO CONSUME WITH CAUTION

The following native plants should either not be consumed at all or at least not consumed on a regular basis due to potential health risks.

## MILKWEEDS
*Asclepias tuberosa* (pictured) and 21 other species

There are 21 native *Asclepias* species and 1 naturalized exotic species in Florida. Although many foragers boil the immature pods of milkweeds, pour the water off at least once, and then fry them, I would consider this risky behavior because the edibility and toxicity depend on the species, and all species contain cardiac glycosides that can damage the heart. Milkweeds are toxic to grazing livestock and, when eaten in quantity, can be fatal. They are larval host plants for monarch, queen, and soldier butterflies, but even their larvae are toxic to birds and mammals. Eating any part of milkweeds is a health risk, but the most commonly eaten milkweed is *Asclepias syriaca*, which does not occur in Florida. So do some research and heed the advice of ethnobotanists.

## TEABUSH
*Melochia tomentosa*

Decoctions from the roots and leaves of teabush have traditionally been used for beverages and medicinal herbal teas, but studies have confirmed this species to be carcinogenic and the cause of tumors of the esophagus in people who consumed it frequently.

## SEASIDE HELIOTROPE
*Heliotropium curassavicum*

The leaves of this low-growing coastal species are known to contain alkaloids that have a negative cumulative effect on body organs. A cancer risk was discovered after doctors on the island of Curaçao noticed a high rate of liver cancer among residents, and medical researchers discovered it was due to the frequent consumption of seaside heliotrope.

**FALSE GARLIC**
*Nothoscordum bivalve*

This species is mentioned in the literature as being toxic, so err on the safe side and avoid eating it. Also be cautious and do not mistake it for meadow garlic (*Allium canadense*), described in the edible section of this guide.

## SOUTHERN BRACKEN
*Pteridium aquilinum*

Although the young fiddleheads of this common fern are eaten by some foragers, older leaves are toxic and can kill cattle. More importantly, new medical research suggests that young fiddleheads should not be consumed with any regularity because recent studies indicate they are carcinogenic, so eating the fiddleheads of this fern poses a long-term health risk.

## ROUGE PLANT OR BLOODBERRY
*Rivina humilis*

It would be prudent to not eat the fruits of rouge plant. Dr. Dan Austin (1943–2015), in his book *Florida Ethnobotany*, wrote that botanist D. W. Nellis reported that "consuming the fruits [of rouge plant] causes numbness of the mouth within 2 hours, with a feeling of warmth in the throat and stomach. Those symptoms are followed by coughing, thirst, tiredness with yawning, vomiting, and diarrhea, sometimes bloody." Florida gardeners who like to grow native plants sometimes purposely cultivate this species because birds eat the fruits. It flowers and fruits all year and spreads readily from seeds.

## BLOODROOT
*Sanguinaria canadensis*

While Native Americans used the red, sticky sap from the thick rhizomes to treat warts and other skin lesions, if any part of bloodroot is consumed in quantity it is toxic and potentially deadly. It is also toxic to dogs and horses that eat the leaves. The USDA has warnings against its consumption, so it is best to simply admire the pretty flowers.

## AMERICAN BLACK NIGHTSHADE
*Solanum americanum*

All parts of American black nightshade contain highly toxic glycoalkaloids, especially the green, unripe fruits, which have caused the deaths of children. Also, the leaves and stems contain high nitrate levels that can kill grazing live-stock. Although the fully ripe (black) fruits are frequently eaten by foragers, and even regarded as "delicious to eat raw and make excellent jams," ripe fruits still reportedly contain low levels of glycoalkaloids and, if eaten in quantity, can cause severe diarrhea and cardiac arrest. So my advice is to eat them in moderation or not at all.

# A WORD ABOUT MUSHROOMS

Mushrooms have been omitted from this guide because they require an entirely different skill set to properly identify, and the only way a person can be certain if a mushroom is edible or potentially deadly is to properly identify it. This requires becoming familiar with the different families of mushrooms, gaining confidence at identifying them in the field, and then knowing a mycologist who can positively confirm your identification. I will refer the reader to the book *Common Florida Mushrooms*, in the references section of this guide.

# Edible and Medicinal Wild Plants

Plants in this section are arranged alphabetically by plant family so foragers can gain a better understanding about which species are related to one another, but be advised that some species within a particular plant family might be edible while others may be mildly or dangerously toxic.

# AGAVACEAE (AGAVE FAMILY)

## SPANISH BAYONET
*Yucca aloifolia*

**Also called:** Aloe yucca, dagger plant
**Nativity:** Native
**Florida range:** Throughout most of coastal Florida
**Habitat:** Coastal dunes and shell mounds
**Description:** Solitary or clumping with upright trunks that typically reach 8'–12' tall and surrounded with dark green, sharp-tipped, narrowly lanceolate leaves reaching 16" long and 2" wide. Flower spikes are terminal, bearing somewhat conical, pendent, white flowers to about 2" long.
**Cautions:** Be extremely careful around this plant because the leaves terminate in a very sharp tip that can cause puncture wounds, and are especially dangerous to children and pets from stab wounds to the eyes, which can cause permanent loss of eyesight. If you grow Spanish bayonet, take a pair of garden shears and snip off the sharp leaf tips, at least on the leaves that are at or below eye level.
**Comments:** In the Caribbean, this species is frequently planted along property lines to create a formidable privacy fence. Harvesting the flowers in the field might prove difficult because the flower spike is terminal and may be far out of reach without a ladder or an extendable limb saw.
**Uses:** The flower petals can be picked and eaten, added to salads, sautéed, roasted, or dipped in batter and fried. The petals can also be dipped in whisked egg whites or melted butter, coated with confectioners' sugar, dried, and eaten as candy. Harvest fresh, new flowers because possible bitterness may be due to the age of the flowers.

# ADAM'S NEEDLE
## *Yucca filamentosa*

**Also called:** Beargrass, desert candle
**Nativity:** Native
**Florida range:** Across Florida south to Lee and Broward Counties
**Habitat:** Sandhills, dunes, coastal scrub, and other open, sunny, sandy habitats, including disturbed sites
**Description:** A stemless species forming a rosette of flat, linear-lanceolate leaves with long curling fibers attached to the leaf margins. Leaves typically reach 24"–36" long and 3"–4" wide. Flower spikes are often twice the height of the plant, reaching 6' tall or more. Pendent flowers are white and reach about 2"–2¾" long.
**Cautions:** The roots contain saponins and should not be eaten. The leaves have sharply pointed tips that can cause puncture wounds to the skin and eyes of humans and pets.
**Comments:** The flowers are easier to harvest than Spanish bayonet because they are not produced high and out of reach. This is a plant typically found in sandhill and scrub habitats but can sometimes be found as an unwanted plant in pastures where livestock graze. The landowner will likely be happy if you offer to dig some plants up for their roots to make soap. Moundlily yucca (*Yucca gloriosa*) also occurs in Florida and is a state-listed endangered species. They all have similar flowers.
**Uses:** The flowers have the same uses as Spanish bayonet, described above, but many people find them to be bitter, so try harvesting a few when they are young and fresh. The leaf fibers have been used to make rope or string, both by Native Americans and early settlers, and the fibers are used by birds in nest building. The roots can be dried, peeled, cut into cubes, and mashed to produce a saponin-laced soap to wash your hair. Conduct a test with the soap on your skin first to ensure you do not have an irritating reaction to it.

# AIZOACEAE (CARPETWEED FAMILY)

## SHORELINE SEAPURSLANE
*Sesuvium portulacastrum*

**Also called:** Cencilla
**Nativity:** Native
**Florida range:** Coastal counties of Florida, including the Florida Keys
**Habitat:** Coastal shorelines and salt marshes
**Description:** Herbaceous perennial with long, succulent stems that spread across the ground, often rooting at the nodes. The succulent, opposite, elliptic to oblanceolate leaves average 1"–1½" long and about ⅜"–⁷⁄₁₆" wide. Star-shaped, pink to nearly white flowers are ½" wide.
**Cautions:** The juice from crushed leaves is salty and can irritate the eyes.
**Comments:** This is a frequent plant in saline habitats, often forming carpets of stems and leaves. Another Florida native species called slender seapurslane (*Sesuvium maritimum*) is much smaller, far less frequent, and has small, white flowers.
**Uses:** The leaves can be boiled with several changes of water to reduce their saltiness and served as a potherb. The leaves can also be eaten raw as a salty snack while hiking, chopped and added to salads, or added to soups or stews as a substitute for salt.

## DESERT HORSEPURSLANE
*Trianthema portulacastrum*

**Also called:** Pigweed
**Nativity:** Native
**Florida range:** Vouchered in Flagler, Seminole, Hillsborough, Manatee, Palm Beach, and Miami-Dade Counties and in mainland Monroe County and the Monroe County Keys
**Habitat:** Mostly disturbed coastal sites
**Description:** Herbaceous annual with prostrate or ascending, pinkish, succulent stems averaging 12"–16" tall. The paired, succulent leaves are suborbicular to obovate and reach 1"–2" long and ¾"–1½" wide, with one leaf in the pair larger than the other. Pink, axillary flowers are solitary or in clusters of 3 per axil, measuring about ½" wide.
**Cautions:** Older leaves of this species have been implicated in causing diarrhea and even mild paralysis, so only harvest the tender young leaves. The seeds are considered to be harmful contaminants in harvested crop seeds and grains. The juice from crushed leaves is salty and can irritate the eyes.
**Comments:** This species is native across the southern United States, tropical America, the West Indies, and Africa.
**Uses:** The fresh, young leaves can be eaten raw as a salty snack or prepared the same as shoreline seapurslane, described above. Dried leaves are widely used medicinally throughout its global range, especially for their beneficial effects to the liver. See Cautions regarding eating older, mature leaves of this species.

# ALLIACEAE (GARLIC FAMILY)

## MEADOW GARLIC
*Allium canadense* var. *canadense* and *A. canadense* var. *mobilense*

**Also called:** Wild garlic, wild onion, Canadian garlic
**Nativity:** Native
**Florida range:** *Allium canadense* var. *canadense* ranges across the Florida Panhandle into south-central Florida, while var. *mobilense* (pictured) ranges across the Florida Panhandle into Alachua County.
**Habitat:** Moist thickets, open fields, and roadsides
**Description:** Narrow, grass-like leaves range 6"–12" long, arising from an underground bulb. Flower stalks are topped by a cluster of pale pink, fragrant flowers, appearing in spring. *Allium canadense* var. *canadense* rarely produces seeds, spreading mostly by bulbils.
**Cautions:** It can become weedy in cultivation. Be certain to not mistake this species for crow-poison (*Nothoscordum bivalve*). See the section in this guide on native plants to avoid eating.
**Comments:** Like its species name implies, *Allium canadense* ranges northward into Canada and also occurs across much of the United States, but var. *mobilense* is only found in the southeastern United States. It is sometimes included in the Amaryllis family (Amaryllidaceae).
**Uses:** The leaves can be chopped and used like chives, and the underground bulbs can be eaten raw, chopped and added to salads, or cooked in the same manner as onions.

# AMARANTHACEAE (AMARANTH FAMILY)

## SOUTHERN AMARANTH
*Amaranthus australis*

**Also called:** Southern water-hemp
**Nativity:** Native
**Florida range:** Throughout the Florida peninsula, with voucher specimens from the south-central Panhandle and Escambia County
**Habitat:** Freshwater and brackish wetlands but often found as a weed in irrigated croplands and residential areas
**Description:** Herbaceous annual that may reach 8'–10' tall with a hollow main stem that can reach 6" in diameter at the base, although plants may mature and flower when only 24" tall

or less. The lower half of the stem is usually reddish in color, becoming green midway up the stem. Leaves are typically narrowly ovate, measuring 3"–8" long and up to 2" wide, with smooth margins. Linear flowering spikes are usually at the top of the stems, with separate male and female flowers. Small seeds are reddish brown to dark brown.

**Cautions:** Amaranth leaves are high in oxalates so they should be eaten in moderation, especially for those who are prone to kidney stones. Another species, *Amaranthus spinosus*, has sharp spines on the stems.

**Comments:** Amaranth species have been widely consumed as greens (cooked or raw), and the seeds have been ground into flour by various cultures around the world for centuries. Of the 15 species of *Amaranthus* in Florida, only 4 species are native, with *Amaranthus floridanus* being endemic to Florida. The leaves and seeds are high in fiber and protein as well as essential amino acids and vitamins.

**Uses:** Young, tender leaves and stems of southern amaranth are commonly eaten as greens (raw, boiled, or stir-fried), and the seeds are ground into flour, boiled to make tea, fermented to make beer, or heated until they pop open and then mixed with sugar to make a sweet confection. Amaranth flowers can also be brewed into a tea that is popular in parts of Asia.

## SPINY AMARANTH
*Amaranthus spinosus*

**Also called:** Spiny pigweed, stickerweed

**Nativity:** Introduced

**Florida range:** Throughout all of Florida

**Habitat:** Mostly disturbed sites, especially as a weed in farm fields but also occasionally as a weed in home landscapes

**Description:** An erect, often much-branched herbaceous annual with pairs of sharp spines in the leaf nodes along the stems. It can reach 5' tall but is usually only half that height. Leaves are lanceolate to ovate, measuring 1"–3" long and ½"–1½" wide. Tiny male and female flowers are borne separately on axillary and terminal spikes. Very small, black seeds are produced by the thousands on a single plant (up to 235,000).

**Cautions:** Beware of the very sharp spines on the stems. The plant is allegedly toxic to grazing livestock such as sheep, cattle, and goats, but most animals avoid it due to the spines.

**Comments:** This species is generally thought of as a nuisance due to its prolific seed production and its sharp spines, yet it is a major food source for peasants in many developing countries, where it is sometimes seen for sale in marketplaces. This is not a species to purposely cultivate due to its weediness and sharp spines. It is listed in the top 20 of the world's worst agricultural weeds.

**Uses:** The tender new leaves can be cooked and eaten as greens and are high in protein, beta carotene, calcium, potassium, and iron. The seeds can be ground into a form of flour, which can be used to thicken gravy or soups, or to add to pancake batter or biscuit dough. It has some medicinal uses to treat fever, excessive menstruation, urinary troubles, diarrhea, and nosebleeds, plus the crushed leaves have been proven to be effective for soothing and healing minor burns.

## SAMPHIRE
*Blutaparon vermiculare (*formerly *Philoxerus vermicularis)*

**Also called:** Silverhead, beach carpet, beach samphire
**Nativity:** Native
**Florida range:** Duval and Levy Counties south along both coasts into the Florida Keys
**Habitat:** Coastal dunes, salt marshes, rocky shorelines, and fringes of mangrove forests
**Description:** Prostrate, succulent perennial with ascending branches lined with thick, linear-lanceolate or oblanceolate leaves that average 1"–2" long and about ⅜" wide. Small, yellow flowers appear in silvery-white heads at the branch tips.
**Cautions:** The salty juice from the leaves can irritate the eyes.
**Comments:** This species can form extensive mats in coastal habitats, often near mangroves or along beaches. It is the namesake of Samphire Key in Florida Bay within Everglades National Park.
**Uses:** The succulent leaves can be picked and eaten as a salty snack, chopped and added to salads, or cooked as a pre-salted potherb. The chopped leaves can also be added to soups, stews, or rice dishes as a salty flavoring.

# ANACARDIACEAE (CASHEW FAMILY)

## MANGO
*Mangifera indica*

**Also called:** There are more than a hundred named cultivars in the global nursery trade, with some of the more popular varieties in Florida being Carrie, Fairchild, Glenn, Haden, Julie, Keitt, Kent, Nam Doc Mai, and Valencia Pride.

**Nativity:** Introduced from Asia

**Florida range:** Naturalized from Brevard and Pinellas Counties south through the coastal counties into the Florida Keys

**Habitat:** Hammocks and disturbed sites, often near groves or residential areas where it is cultivated

**Description:** Tree to 30' or more with narrowly lanceolate leaves averaging 6"–8" long and 1½"–2" wide. Small, yellow flowers are in terminal panicles and are followed by oblong to sub-reniform fruits ranging about 4½"–6½" long and 2½"–3½" wide. The fruits ripen from green to either yellow or red and yellow. The flesh is yellow to orange-yellow.

**Cautions:** Some unfortunate people are allergic to the sap and break out with a skin rash exactly like the reaction from the related poison ivy (*Toxicodendron radicans*) and poison-wood (*Metopium toxiferum*). Those who are allergic to the sap can usually eat the flesh without a reaction, but they must have someone else peel them.

**Comments:** Wild mango trees in Florida are the result of them growing from seed, either discarded by humans or carried there by raccoons, opossums, or other animals. Because they have grown from seed, their fruits will typically not be as tasty as on the cultivated tree they came from, often being stringy with a flavor reminiscent of turpentine, but still worth eating.

**Uses:** There is nothing better than to simply peel and eat a ripe mango. If you plan to eat a whole peeled fruit out of hand, it's best to do so in the shower because the juice will cover your hands and face and drip off your chin. As with other non-native naturalized fruit trees, if you find a fruiting mango tree growing wild, take the seeds out with you to avoid contributing to its spread. There are countless dishes made from mangoes, ranging from pies to smoothies to fruit salads.

# WINGED SUMAC
*Rhus copallinum*

**Also called:** Southern sumac, shining sumac
**Nativity:** Native
**Florida range:** Throughout all of Florida
**Habitat:** Pinelands, rocky or sandy upland forests, woodland borders, savannas, limestone glades, fencerows, and abandoned fields
**Description:** Winged sumac is typically a shrubby species but can reach 20' tall or more. The compound leaves are characterized by a winged rachis (leaf stem). Leaflets are lanceolate, averaging 2"–3" long and ⅜"–½" wide, turning red in winter. Pale yellow flowers are in terminal clusters; and on female plants, these are followed by dense clusters of round, ⅛" fruits that ripen dull red.
**Cautions:** Poison sumac (*Toxicodendron vernix*) occurs in central and northern Florida but does not have wings on the leaf stem between the leaflets. It is closely related to poison ivy (*Toxicodendron radicans*) and contains the same toxin (urushiol) that causes contact dermatitis.

**Comments:** Winged sumac is common in a variety of habitats, sometimes forming thickets. Male and female flowers are borne on separate plants.

**Uses:** Clusters of fruits can be picked, washed, and cooked over low heat for about 10 minutes and then allowed to steep for up to 30 minutes to make a tasty tea that resembles pink lemonade in flavor. Before serving, it is best to pour the water through a coffee filter to remove any hairs or other impurities from the fruits. Add some sugar or honey to sweeten and a squeeze of lime if you'd like. Serve warm or on ice. Winged sumac tea was used medicinally by Native Americans for treating diarrhea and later by settlers to control blood sugar levels. The small fruits are high in Vitamin A and can be eaten fresh but are somewhat tart or sour-tasting, depending on their degree of ripeness.

# ANNONACEAE (CUSTARD APPLE FAMILY)

## POND APPLE
*Annona glabra*

**Also called:** Alligator apple
**Nativity:** Native
**Florida range:** From Brevard, Highlands, and Manatee Counties south into the Florida Keys
**Habitat:** Freshwater sloughs, mixed hardwood swamps, and in deep solution holes within tropical hardwood hammocks
**Description:** Small, spreading, deciduous tree to 25' tall or less, often multi-trunked and buttressed at the base, with leathery, ovate to elliptic leaves reaching 5" long and 3" wide. Pendent flowers have 3 leathery, creamy-white petals with a red blotch on the inner base. The ovoid fruits average about 4" long and 3" wide, ripening yellow and containing numerous brown seeds.

**Cautions:** The peeled bark and sawdust have caused dermatitis on sensitive people, and getting the powder from ground seeds into the eyes may cause irritation and temporary blindness. Ground seeds can kill small fish when placed in water. This tree is typically found where cottonmouth moccasins reside, so watch your step.

**Comments:** Besides bearing edible fruits, the soft wood has been used for fishing floats and bottle corks, and crushed leaves have been placed in hen nests to kill lice.

**Uses:** Although the flavor of pond apple fruits is disappointing when compared to the related neotropical cherimoya (*Annona cherimola*), custard apple (*Annona reticulata*), sugar apple (*Annona squamosa*), and soursop or guanabana (*Annona muricata*), a ripe pond apple is perfectly edible eaten out of hand and made into pies or even desserts. For pies, simply replace the apples in an apple pie recipe with pond apple pulp after first peeling the fruits and removing the seeds. Or, combine apples and pond apple in a traditional apple pie recipe. For a refreshing dessert, place the pulp of half a ripe pond apple fruit into a glass, add sugar to taste, and then fill the rest of the glass with shaved ice. Stir to combine the ingredients and enjoy with a spoon. For foragers in the field, simply peel and eat ripe fruits and spit out the seeds.

## BIGFLOWER PAWPAW
*Asimina obovata*

**Also called:** Scrub pawpaw, flag pawpaw
**Nativity:** Native
**Florida range:** Endemic to peninsular Florida from Levy, Alachua, Clay, and Flagler Counties south to Hillsborough, Polk, Glades, and St. Lucie Counties
**Habitat:** Pine-oak woods, sandhills, dry pinelands, scrub, and occasionally coastal dunes
**Description:** Woody shrub to about 9' tall with leathery, obovate, oblong, or ovate leaves averaging 2"–4" long and half as wide. Large, showy, white flowers have a lemon-like fragrance and appear on the new shoots after the leaves appear.
**Cautions:** Pawpaws contain compounds that are known to cause skin rashes on sensitive people simply from handling the fruits, so if you have never handled pawpaw fruits before, do so with due caution until you know they are safe for you to handle. Seeds of pawpaws are emetic and may cause vomiting if eaten.

**Comments:** This species is endemic to the central peninsula of Florida where it is found in well-drained sandy soils of scrub and sandhill habitats. It has large fruits, second in size only to *Asimina triloba*, a tree that ranges south into the central Panhandle and is the species most commonly eaten, but the fruits of *Asimina obovata* are known to have been a popular food item for indigenous tribes and settlers within its restricted range. There are 12 native *Asimina* species in Florida, along with an additional 6 named hybrids, and all have edible fruits. Pawpaw fruits are sometimes available in roadside stands in northern Florida, or are available online in season.

**Uses:** Ripe fruits can be picked, peeled, and eaten fresh, added to salsa, blended as a beverage, or used to bake breads and pies.

## RECIPE

**Pawpaw Salsa**

Pawpaw fruits, peeled, seeded, and chopped
Tomatoes, chopped
Scallion, finely chopped with leaves
Jalapeño pepper, finely chopped
Cilantro, chopped
Juice of a lime or lemon

Simply add the above ingredients in a bowl, toss, and serve as a salsa with tortilla chips. The amount of each ingredient is up to you. Other fruits, such as mangoes, avocados, bananas, blueberries, or peaches can be added, as well as garlic, bell peppers, or whatever else you'd like. If you prefer peppers hotter than jalapeños, then go for it!

# NETTED PAWPAW
*Asimina reticulata*

**Also called:** Dog apple, Seminole tea, flatwoods pawpaw

**Nativity:** Native

**Florida range:** Throughout much of peninsular Florida but absent in the northernmost counties, including the Panhandle

**Habitat:** Scrub, sandhills, and pine flatwoods

**Description:** This shrubby species typically reaches about 4' in height but may be taller. The oblong, fleshy leaves average 1½"–4" long and 1" wide, with netted venation and orange hairs. The outer petals are creamy white, sometimes with pale brown lines, and measure about 1½" long and 1" wide. The 1½"–1¾" cylindrical fruits are yellowish green when ripe.

**Cautions:** The state- and federal-listed endangered fourpetal pawpaw (*Asimina tetramera*) is endemic to Martin and Palm Beach Counties and should not be harvested due to its protected status. Also, read the Cautions section for the previous species because they apply to this and other species as well.

**Comments:** Look for ripe fruits of netted pawpaw from May to early summer. Curiously, Dr. Dan Austin (1943–2015) wrote that despite the common name "Seminole tea," there is no record of the Seminole tribe using this species for tea or anything else, even though they almost assuredly ate the fruits.

**Uses:** The flesh of ripe fruits of all species can be eaten fresh, but some are clearly better tasting than others.

# APIACEAE (CARROT FAMILY)

## COASTAL PLAIN ANGELICA
*Angelica dentata*

**Also called:** Sandhill angelica
**Nativity:** Native
**Florida range:** From Leon and Wakulla Counties west to Bay and Jackson Counties in the Florida Panhandle. It also ranges into Georgia where it is considered rare.
**Habitat:** Pinelands, sandhills, and bogs
**Description:** Perennial herb to about 36" tall. Compound leaves have long petioles that clasp the stem, and each leaf is divided into several coarsely toothed and deeply divided, leathery leaflets. The leaves are typically few in number. Small, white flowers are in flat-topped clusters, each divided into numerous small clusters.
**Cautions:** There is a possibility of mistaking species of *Angelica* with the very poisonous spotted water hemlock (*Cicuta maculata*). Also, women should avoid consuming tea made from the roots of any *Angelica* species during pregnancy because it may induce uterine contractions.

**Comments:** A second native species of *Angelica* in the Florida Panhandle is hairy angelica (*Angelica venenosa*), with hairy leaves. Although the species name translates to "very poisonous," this came about when it was first described in 1793 from plants collected in Virginia and was mistaken for a species of *Cicuta* (water hemlock), thus given the name *Cicuta venenosa*. It was later determined that it was a species of *Angelica*, but due to the rules of botanical nomenclature, the unfortunate species name had to be retained even though the plant is not poisonous. In Europe, members of this genus are considered holy because the flowers religiously open during the feast of St. Michael the Archangel. Candied roots are popular in Europe.

**Uses:** All parts are edible. The seeds can be ground and used as a spice; the leaves can be eaten raw, cooked, or chopped and added as a flavoring for poultry, fish, or other meats; and the tender young stems can be eaten raw, cooked, or candied. Angelica has been described as resembling juniper berries or licorice in flavor and makes a flavorful herbal tea that can have a stimulating effect on the digestive system. The very hard roots can be washed and grated, then used to flavor gin, white rum, or vodka or boiled with sugar to make a syrup, but many foraging enthusiasts deem using the roots to not be worth the effort.

## RECIPE

**Candied Angelica Stems**

1. Cut young, tender angelica stems into 3" lengths.

2. Bring equal parts of water and sugar to a boil and add the angelica stems. Lower heat and simmer 4–5 minutes. Remove the stems and dunk them in ice water, retaining the sugar syrup in the pot.

3. Peel the skin off the stems with a sharp knife, place the stems in a bowl, then pour the sugar syrup over them before placing the bowl in the refrigerator overnight.

4. Repeat Step 2 twice more over the next 2 days.

5. After this process is finished on the third day, remove the stems, pat them dry with a paper towel, then sprinkle with granulated sugar (brown sugar is best).

# AQUIFOLIACEAE (HOLLY FAMILY)

## DAHOON
*Ilex cassine*

**Also called:** Cassine, dahoon holly
**Nativity:** Native
**Florida range:** Throughout all of mainland Florida (absent from the Florida Keys)
**Habitat:** Pinelands and hardwood forest margins
**Description:** Small, dioecious, evergreen tree to 20' tall or more with an 8'–12' spread. Alternate leaves are elliptical, from 2"–4" long and half as wide, with entire margins or with a few teeth along the forward half of the blade. Small, white to greenish-white flowers have 4 lobes and measure about ¼" across, followed by oval fruits to about ¼" wide and produced in showy clusters on female trees.

**Cautions:** Tea brewed from the leaves has been known to cause dizziness and diarrhea in some people. When eaten in quantity, the fruits are mildly toxic to adults and somewhat more toxic for children.

**Comments:** Although this is the least popular holly for brewing tea, the leaves are air-dried, roasted, and sold for tea in parts of its native range, especially in the southern states.

**Uses:** Pick a half-dozen leaves and allow them to dry for a week or longer, then roast under low heat in an oven. Crumble the dried leaves in a cup of boiling water, allowing them to steep for about 10 minutes. Add sugar or honey if desired.

## GALLBERRY
*Ilex glabra*

**Also called:** Inkberry
**Nativity:** Native
**Florida range:** Throughout all of mainland Florida (absent from the Florida Keys)
**Habitat:** Pinelands, deciduous forests, and hammocks
**Description:** Mounding, evergreen, dioecious shrub, reaching 6'–12' tall and wide, often forming extensive colonies by root suckers. Elliptical to lanceolate, alternate leaves average 1"–2" long and half as wide, varying from light to dark green. White, 5-lobed flowers measure about ¼" across and produce oval, ⅜" fruits that ripen black.
**Cautions:** The fruits are bitter and can be somewhat toxic if eaten in quantity. A low percentage of people experience an upset stomach and/or diarrhea from drinking the tea, so if this tea is new to you, try a few sips and see if it agrees with you or not.
**Comments:** Tea made from the leaves of gallberry is popular and widely consumed, tasting very much like commercial black tea.
**Uses:** The leaves can be air-dried, slow-roasted in an oven with low heat, then crushed and steeped in hot water for several minutes to make a tea that has no caffeine.

# YAUPON HOLLY
*Ilex vomitoria*

**Also called:** Cassina
**Nativity:** Native
**Florida range:** Central and northern peninsular Florida west through the Panhandle
**Habitat:** Sandhills, maritime forests, coastal and inland marshes, and dunes
**Description:** Dioecious, evergreen shrub or small tree to 20' tall, bearing alternate, ovate to elliptical leaves with scalloped or coarsely toothed margins and a rounded tip. The leaves measure ½"–1½" long and ½"–¾" wide. The small, white flowers are 4-lobed and produce oval, glossy, red fruits averaging about ¼" wide.
**Cautions:** The fruits are inedible, bitter, and toxic if eaten in quantity.
**Comments:** Native American tribes made an extra-strong tea from the dried leaves, called "black drink," which was consumed by tribal men during ritualistic ceremonies that involved vomiting, though modern research indicates that the vomiting was caused by the volume of the concentrated and highly caffeinated tea they drank, coupled with fasting. It is allegedly one of only 2 plants native to North America with leaves that contain caffeine (the other is *Ilex cassine*, with much lower levels of caffeine). Strong yaupon tea has been brewed and used medicinally as a laxative.
**Uses:** Pick a cup or so of leaves and allow them to dry for a few days until they are crisp and break apart easily. This is best accomplished by spreading the leaves out on a flat surface with good ventilation. Bryon White of Yaupon Brothers American Tea Company in

Edgewater, Florida, suggests not oven-drying the leaves because it makes the tea taste bitter. Once the leaves have dried naturally, put them in a blender or food processor to break the leaves up into small, ⅛" pieces. You can either place the ground leaves directly into a cup before filling it with boiling water, or place the ground leaves into a metal tea infuser, available in most kitchen appliance stores, and drop it into the cup. A third option is to make your own tea bags. Let the tea steep for several hours and then dilute it with twice the amount of water before straining and serving. Yaupon tea is normally consumed hot or cold without added sweetener, so try it first before adding sugar or honey. *Note:* If you want flavored tea, add mint, hibiscus, or other commercial teas to the yaupon leaves before adding the boiling water. If you want uncaffeinated yaupon tea, pour out the first cup of water and add more boiling water to the cup, then allow it to steep again (most of the caffeine is released into the water the first time). You can also watch a video from the Yaupon Brothers for at-home instructions, including how to make your own tea bags, at https://youtu.be/XzLbyRl6mFc.

# ARECACEAE (PALM FAMILY)

## COCONUT PALM
*Cocos nucifera*

**Nativity:** Introduced
**Florida range:** Cultivated and naturalized in central and southern Florida
**Habitat:** Coastal dunes, disturbed sites, dump piles, or anywhere near mature specimens
**Description:** Single-trunked palm to 30' tall or more, often arching (especially on coastal dunes), and topped with a head of pinnate leaves reaching 10' long or longer. Fruits average about 8"–12" long and 6"–7" wide.
**Cautions:** Falling coconuts are a hazard. Death by falling coconuts has been recorded as early as 1777, and warning signs of their hazard are posted on beaches in Hawaii, Australia, Polynesia, and elsewhere.
**Comments:** The coconut is the most well-known palm in the world and was a godsend to early sailors exploring the world's oceans because the coconuts could be stored in the ship's hold for long periods of time without refrigeration. The nutritious coconut "meat" could be eaten fresh or dried, plus the coconut water inside the seed provided a nutritious beverage. The shell could be cut in half with a saw and used as a cup for drinking, and the dried husk could be burned for cooking. The flesh can also be processed into coconut oil, used in

cooking, and the leaf segments can be woven into hats and skirts. In Florida the coconut palm is listed as a Category II invasive species by the Florida Invasive Species Council, mostly due to it spreading from coconuts germinating along undisturbed beach dunes. The coconuts float and can be carried by ocean currents to shorelines far away from the parent palm. It is believed to be native to Polynesia and nearby Pacific islands but was purposely planted by early explorers along sailing routes as a source of food and drink during future voyages.

**Uses:** The flesh of the coconut can be eaten fresh, dried, or shredded and is used in a wide variety of dishes. There are 3 "eyes" on a coconut seed, and a sharp knife or a drill can be used to hollow one of them out to access the coconut water inside. The delicious and nutritious water can be consumed fresh out of the nut or used in cooking. The coconut water is particularly tasty from immature coconuts. In the Bahamas, coconut water is used to make a popular alcoholic beverage that is simply called gin and coconut water. There is even a song titled "Gin and Coconut Water," sung by a Bahamian band called Baha Men.

## CABBAGE PALM
*Sabal palmetto*

**Also called:** Sabal palm
**Nativity:** Native
**Florida range:** Throughout all of Florida
**Habitat:** Ubiquitous in a wide variety of habitats, including pinelands, coastal strand, dunes, inland and coastal forests, swamps, pastures, and disturbed sites
**Description:** Thick-trunked palm to 45' tall with costapalmate leaves, often with persistent leaf bases on the trunk, and with long, unarmed petioles. Leaf blades are curved downward and measure 3'–4' wide with lax leaf segments. Fragrant flowers are yellowish in dense panicles. Globose fruits ripen black and average ⅜" wide.
**Cautions:** Remember that harvesting hearts of palm kills the palm and is considered illegal unless it is growing on private land and you have the landowner's permission to harvest it.
**Comments:** This is Florida's state tree, and also the state tree of South Carolina, although most dendrologists do not consider palms to be trees. Regardless, the cabbage palm is well-known in Florida, not only as a common species seen in a wide variety of habitats, but also as a popular landscape palm throughout the state. The fronds were commonly used

by indigenous people in Florida to make body coverings for men and women, and the Seminole and Miccosukee would later popularize the use of cabbage palm fronds to make thatched huts called *chickees*, and fronds are still today used in that manner. The threadlike fibers on the fronds are used by a wide variety of birds in nest building. A principal use by Native Americans and settlers in Florida was harvesting the heart of palm as a nutritious food that has been compared to cabbage in flavor, and gave rise to the name, cabbage palm. The canned or bottled hearts of palm sold in grocery stores come from the peach palm (*Bactris gasipaes*), native to Central and South America and cultivated for commercial harvest.

**Uses:** The "heart" of cabbage palm is edible and nutritious, although harvesting it kills the palm because you must chop through the base of the crown with a machete, or cut through it with a chain saw. Please note that the State of Florida has designated the cabbage palm a protected species in order to avoid wholesale harvesting in natural habitats for commercial exploitation, but it can still be legally harvested from areas slated to be cleared for development, or from palms felled by tropical storms or hurricanes. Once the crown has been cut off, continue removing the outer leaf stems until you have reached the center core of the new growth. The heart from a mature palm will be 1'–2' feet long and about 2"–3" across. It can be eaten raw, diced into salads, boiled, baked, or sautéed.

# SAW PALMETTO
*Serenoa repens*

**Also called:** Palmetto, saw palm
**Nativity:** Native
**Florida range:** Throughout all of Florida
**Habitat:** Besides pinelands, saw palmetto inhabits beach dunes, scrub, sandhills, and margins of hardwood forests.
**Description:** A clustering palm with reclining or ascending, branching trunks topped with deeply divided, palmate leaf blades to about 24" wide at the end of long petioles armed with saw-like teeth. Fragrant, yellow flowers are massed on arching, branched stems and are followed by oblong, 2" fruits that begin green then turn orangish-yellow before ripening black.
**Cautions:** Sharp teeth line the petioles (leaf stems) and can cut through exposed skin like a saw. Watch for eastern diamondback rattlesnakes in its habitat because saw palmettos are a favorite place for them to hang out in the shade. The unripe fruits are toxic and should not be eaten. When saw palmetto fruits are ripe, they are a favorite food of Florida black bears, so pay attention when in saw palmetto country.

**Comments:** This palm is well-known in Florida because it is a very common species throughout mainland Florida. It occurs in a variety of habitats, including beach dunes, and is the common understory palm in the pinelands of mainland Florida. The fruits are harvested (often illegally) for the pharmaceutical trade and then processed and sold in tablet form to help men maintain a healthy prostate. A saw palmetto leaf blade is the symbol of the Florida Native Plant Society.

**Uses:** Ripe fruits can be picked and eaten (see Cautions) and were an important food in the diet of Native Americans of the southeastern United States, but the ripe fruits have been unappealingly described as tasting like "rotten cheese steeped in tobacco juice" or "intense blue cheese mixed with gastric juice." The heart of saw palmetto is edible and nutritious, but harvesting it kills the trunk from which it was taken. The good news about saw palmetto is that it is a multi-trunked species, so harvesting the heart from one trunk does not kill the entire cluster. A very sharp machete will be needed to chop through the crown of the trunk, which is then chopped lengthwise to remove the leaf stems and outer trunk. The "heart" is the central growth where new leaves are formed. Harvesting the heart of saw palmetto should be reserved for areas where the palms are destined to be bulldozed for development.

# FLORIDA THATCH PALM
*Thrinax radiata*

**Also called:** Jamaica Thatch Palm
**Nativity:** Native
**Florida range:** Collier, Miami-Dade, and Monroe (mainland and Keys) Counties
**Habitat:** Pine rocklands (Big Pine Key), hammocks, and coastal strand
**Description:** Single-trunked palm from 12' to 20' tall with a crown of palmate leaves, green above and below, measuring 3'–4' wide. The petioles on this and other members of the genus are forked at the base, distinguishing it from the South Florida native silver palm (*Coccothrinax argentata*), which are not forked and on which the undersides of the leaves are silvery. Flowers are white in drooping inflorescences, followed by white fruits to about ¼" wide.
**Cautions:** This is a state-listed endangered species, so harvesting fruits from natural habitats would be unethical, if not illegal, if they are in protected preserves. It is commonly cultivated in South Florida, not only in residential landscapes but also as a street tree and in mall parking lot islands.
**Comments:** The endangered Key thatch palm (*Leucothrinax morrisii*) is similar but with leaf blades that are gray beneath. It occurs in mainland Miami-Dade and Monroe Counties and the Florida Keys. Edibility and cautions are the same as for this species. Both species are commonly sold in South Florida nurseries as a landscape palm.
**Uses:** The white fruits are edible and sweet tasting. The heart, or terminal bud, of this and most other palm species is edible and nutritious, but harvesting it kills the palm. However, it can be harvested in the case of palms being felled by hurricanes or hit by vehicles.

# ASTERACEAE (SUNFLOWER FAMILY)

## OPPOSITELEAF SPOTFLOWER
*Acmella repens (*formerly *Acmella oppositifolia* var. *repens)*

**Also called:** Creeping spotflower (United States), alphabet plant (Brazil)
**Nativity:** Native
**Florida range:** Common throughout much of mainland Florida
**Habitat:** Pinelands, prairies, meadows, depressions, and roadsides
**Description:** This species usually has spreading stems with opposite, toothed leaves measuring ½"–1" wide and flower heads ⅜"–½" wide. The ray florets and the disk are yellow.
**Cautions:** Do not be surprised by the mouth-tingling sensation that comes with eating the flowers of this species.
**Comments:** In Florida, look for this species in short hydroperiod glades, prairie margins, and in pine flatwoods. In Brazil it is called alphabet plant because they believe the tingling of the tongue will make babies speak more easily.
**Uses:** The flowers can be eaten raw and will cause a tingling sensation in your mouth. In South America the flowers are added to soups and stews as a mouth-tingling dining experience. In parts of its native range, the leaves are eaten raw or cooked as a potherb to treat liver disorders and to relieve the pain of sore throat and mouth sores.

# COMMON RAGWEED
*Ambrosia artemisiifolia*

**Also called:** Annual ragweed
**Nativity:** Native
**Florida range:** Throughout all of Florida
**Habitat:** Disturbed sites, especially agricultural fields, scraped areas, roadsides, and trail margins
**Description:** Annual herbaceous species with erect stems typically reaching 24"–30" tall and bearing both alternate and opposite, pinnately lobed leaves with entire or toothed margins. Male (staminate) and female (pistillate) flower heads are produced on the same plant, producing small, rounded, brown seeds.
**Cautions:** This species is a major source of summertime allergies due to airborne pollen. It is sold in pellet form as a homeopathic treatment for ragweed allergies, but consult a medical doctor to see if it is proven to be effective or not.
**Comments:** Purposely cultivating common ragweed is a bad idea because, once established, it is exceptionally difficult to eradicate due to prolific seed set, plus being a major source of seasonal allergies when it releases pollen into the air.
**Uses:** Native Americans not only rubbed the leaves on insect stings, poison ivy rash, and hives, plus crushed the leaves and wiped the juice on skin infections, but they also harvested the abundant seeds as a source of protein, as the seeds are higher in protein than even soybeans. In Cuba the leaves were used in aromatic baths against pain in the joints, muscle pain, and rheumatoid arthritis. The Sioux even used the leaves for toilet paper, perhaps because the leaves are soft. However, a root tea was used as a laxative, so perhaps having a laxative and toilet paper in the same plant was a good thing.

## COASTAL RAGWEED
*Ambrosia hispida*

**Also called:** Bay geranium, bay thyme (Bahamas)

**Nativity:** Native

**Florida range:** Vouchered from coastal regions in Brevard, Lee, Collier, and Miami-Dade Counties, and the Monroe County Keys but likely occurs in other coastal counties of central and southern Florida

**Habitat:** Beach dunes, rocky shorelines, and coastal sandhills

**Description:** Rhizomatous perennial averaging 6"–10" tall, forming spreading colonies. The pinnately lobed leaves are mostly opposite, ovate or elliptic in outline. Flowers are unisexual, with the female (pistillate) heads close to the male (staminate) heads on erect stems 4"–6" tall.

**Cautions:** Some people experience allergic reactions to the airborne pollen, but not as much as the previous species.

**Comments:** This coastal dune species has a long history as bush medicine in the West Indies and tropical America, especially for arthritis, menstrual pain, colds, and influenza. It is often blended with other plants in medicinal decoctions and herbal teas.

**Uses:** A medicinal tea to treat arthritis is made by placing a leaf in a cup, filling the cup with boiling water, and then steeping it for 5 minutes. Sweeten with honey. Tea brewed from fresh leaves is less bitter than dried leaves. In the Bahamas, this herbal tea is taken before bedtime to relieve anxiety and hypertension. A decoction made by boiling the roots is used as a wash to treat fevers and itching skin.

## SPANISH NEEDLES
*Bidens alba (*referred to as *Bidens pilosa* by some taxonomists)*

**Also called:** Beggar ticks, romerillo
**Nativity:** Native
**Florida range:** Common throughout all of Florida
**Habitat:** Mostly disturbed sites, including vacant lots, pastures, canal banks, fencerows, residential landscapes, trail margins, and roadsides
**Description:** Herbaceous annual or perennial that averages 12"–24" tall with leaves to about 2" long, divided into 3 or 5 ovate to lanceolate segments, with toothed margins. The lowermost leaves are frequently undivided. Flower heads measure about 1" across with white ray florets ("petals") and yellow disks. Seeds (achenes) are about ½" long and forked on one end.
**Cautions:** Seeds can be a nuisance because they stick to hair and clothing. If you suffer from hypoglycemia (low blood sugar), then you should avoid eating members of the genus *Bidens* because of a compound that lowers blood sugar levels and acts as a central nervous system depressant.
**Comments:** This is a well-known, ubiquitous weedy species that is often found in home landscapes, where it is either cursed by homeowners or cherished because the flowers attract a multitude of butterflies and it is a larval host plant of the dainty sulphur butterfly.
**Uses:** Young leaves can be eaten raw or cooked as a potherb. The leaves are said to contain 50 percent more available iron than spinach, but they have a somewhat resinous taste, especially if eaten raw. It is best to collect the tender new leaves and soak them in a bowl of water placed in the refrigerator overnight to help eliminate some of the resinous flavor, and then steam or boil the leaves until tender. To further enhance your dining pleasure, add a mixture of olive oil, lemon or lime juice, and grated parmesan or Romano cheese. Minced scallions and tomatoes can also be added to turn it into an interesting side dish at the dinner table. The flower heads can be eaten raw or used as a decorative addition to salads. In addition to its edibility, there are numerous medicinal properties reported in the literature. The warmed juice from the stems will stop bleeding from small cuts, such as nicks from shaving. There are 7 members of the genus native to Florida, including the next species.

## PURPLE THISTLE
*Cirsium horridulum*

**Also called:** Bull thistle, horrid thistle
**Nativity:** Native
**Florida range:** Throughout all of Florida
**Habitat:** Mostly roadsides, canal banks, vacant lots, and other disturbed sites
**Description:** Herbaceous biennial or perennial with coarsely lobed, spiny, linear to oblanceolate leaves produced in a rosette. Flower heads range in color from purple, pinkish purple, yellow, or white, measuring about 2" wide. Seeds are wind dispersed.
**Cautions:** Very sharp spines cover the stems and leaves.
**Comments:** This is a common, weedy species that is seldom purposely cultivated even though the flower heads are visited by butterflies, bees, and even hummingbirds.
**Uses:** Although the spines on the leaves can be cut off with scissors prior to eating raw or cooked, most foragers simply strip the leaf blade off the stem and eat the central leaf stem (midrib). The stout taproots of young plants are edible raw or cooked. Cooking methods include boiling or steaming.

# CANADIAN HORSEWEED
*Conyza canadensis*

**Also called:** Bitterweed, Canadian fleabane, donkey herb (Sinaloa), little skunk feces (New Mexico)

**Nativity:** Considered native in the online Atlas of Florida Plants (as *Erigeron canadensis*) and in *Flora of North America* (as *Conyza canadensis*), but a cosmopolitan weed around the globe

**Florida range:** Throughout all of Florida

**Habitat:** A weed of disturbed sites, especially in agricultural fields

**Description:** Herbaceous annual (rarely biennial) to 7' tall but typically only half that tall or less. The coarsely hairy, erect stem is unbranched until it terminates in branched panicles of small flower heads with white ray florets. Alternate stem leaves are hairy, measuring about ¼" wide and up to 5" long, but becoming smaller as they ascend up the stem. Seeds are wind dispersed.

**Cautions:** This species is exceptionally weedy, so it is not a plant to purposely cultivate, or at least not be allowed to set seed, or you may come up with some new curse words when you're out pulling weeds.

**Comments:** Although this species has been known for decades as *Conyza canadensis*, some botanists have cited recent molecular research that they believe supports moving it into the genus *Erigeron*. One reason that it has become such an agricultural weed is it is resistant to herbicides containing glyphosates. A second species, *Conyza bonariensis*, also occurs in Florida and is used to treat asthma, hence its common name asthmaweed.

**Uses:** Very young basal or seedling leaves can be steamed or boiled and eaten as a pot-herb with an interesting, slightly bitter, spicy flavor. Leaves can also be dried, crumbled, and added to soups and stews to impart a tarragon-like flavor. It has a wide range of medicinal uses throughout its native range as well as in Europe, Africa, and Asia where it has become a naturalized weed. In Florida it has been used by the Seminole tribe to treat coughs and colds, but there is no record of it being used as a food or medicine in the Bahamas. Other tribes of Native Americans in North America used a decoction of the roots and leaves to treat stomach pain, chronic diarrhea, convulsions in children, and "female weakness." Leaves and other plant parts were pounded with rocks and the juice applied to sore joints and to relieve the pain from sprains and backache.

# EASTERN PURPLE CONEFLOWER
*Echinacea purpurea*

**Also called:** Hedgehog flower
**Nativity:** Native
**Florida range:** Vouchered only from Gadsden County in the Florida Panhandle
**Habitat:** Prairies and rocky, open woods
**Description:** Herbaceous, roughly hairy perennial 24"–48" tall with ovate to narrowly lanceolate leaves measuring 2"–10" long and 2"–4" wide, with toothed (serrate) margins and 3–5 prominent nerves. Flowers average about 2"–2½" across with pink to purple ray florets and dark purple to orange-red discs.
**Cautions:** German research has shown a very low ratio of allergic reactions to echinacea products. Avoid purchasing seeds of named cultivars because such plants will be different from native forms.
**Comments:** Modern medical research shows that extracts of the plant stimulate the immune system as a preventive measure for colds, and tea bags of the crushed, dried leaves are sold in supermarkets, pharmacies, and health food stores. It is widely used to prevent and treat upper respiratory tract infections. Native Americans prescribed it for snakebites, stings, toothaches, coughs, venereal disease, burns, flu, colds, and other ailments. Although this is a rare, endangered species in Florida, seeds are available from the Florida Wildflower Foundation and elsewhere.
**Uses:** Leaves can be harvested, dried, crumbled, and steeped in hot water to brew a pleasant herbal tea. Add honey or lemon if desired. The ray florets ("petals") on the flower heads can be picked and eaten.

## SEACOAST MARSHELDER
*Iva imbricata*

**Also called:** Sumpweed
**Nativity:** Native
**Florida range:** Along both coasts of Florida south to the Florida Keys
**Habitat:** Beach dunes
**Description:** The ascending stems of this species average 10"–20" tall and are lined with smooth, succulent leaves from 1"–1½" long to about ⅜" wide, becoming smaller up the stems. Male (staminate) and female (pistillate) flowers are together in the same head and are encased by overlapping bracts.
**Cautions:** Check local ordinances about the legality of harvesting leaves or seeds of plants on public beaches.
**Comments:** There are 4 other native species of *Iva* in Florida, and all have been used as food by indigenous tribes. The seeds have been found to be high in fat, protein, niacin, thiamine, iron, calcium, and phosphorus.
**Uses:** The succulent leaves can be steamed or boiled and served as a green, and the round fruits can be boiled to help make the seeds easier to harvest. The seeds have an agreeable, nutty flavor.

# SWEETSCENT
*Pluchea odorata*

**Also called:** Shrubby camphorweed, saltmarsh fleabane
**Nativity:** Native
**Florida range:** Throughout all of Florida
**Habitat:** Salt or brackish marshes, estuaries, and other coastal habitats; less commonly inland
**Description:** Herbaceous annual or short-lived perennial to 4' tall with alternate, aromatic, ovate to ovate-lanceolate leaves measuring 2"–4" long and 1"–2" wide, becoming smaller above. Flower heads are in flat-topped cymes, each head measuring about ³⁄₁₆" across. Seeds are wind dispersed.
**Cautions:** The leaf tea should be avoided or taken only in moderation during pregnancy.
**Comments:** This is one of several members of the genus with leaves that were placed in bedding to deter fleas, hence the common name fleabane. The leaves of this species are widely used throughout its native range in the West Indies and American tropics as a medicinal herbal tea, both as a stimulant to induce perspiration or to increase menstrual flow. The leaf tea is also used medicinally to treat cramps, muscle spasms, upset stomach, and hay fever.
**Uses:** To brew a medicinal herbal tea (see Cautions), place crushed leaves in a pot of boiling water, remove from heat, and allow to steep for up to 20 minutes. Add sugar or honey if desired. Serve hot or cold.

## SWEET GOLDENROD
*Solidago odora* var. *chapmanii*

**Also called:** Bouhea-tea
**Nativity:** Native
**Florida range:** Throughout all of mainland Florida, with 2 named varieties. *Solidago odora* var. *chapmanii* is found throughout peninsular Florida and has disjunct populations in Bay and Franklin Counties in the Florida Panhandle. *Solidago odora* var. *odora* is found across northern Florida west throughout the Panhandle.
**Habitat:** Pinelands, prairies, flatwoods, and margins of forests
**Description:** Erect to arching herbaceous perennial reaching 24"–48" when flowering. The leaves are usually anise-scented, though more distinctly with var. *odora* than var. *chapmanii*. The stem leaves measure 1¼"–2¾" long and ⅜"–⅝" wide and are often slightly twisted. The stems on var. *chapmanii* are uniformly covered with fine pubescence, while the pubescence on the stems of var. *odora* is in lines or strips along the stems, but you will need a hand lens

or magnifying glass to observe this feature clearly. Yellow flowers are arranged on branched terminal stalks. Seeds are wind dispersed.

**Cautions:** There is a common belief that goldenrods are a source of hay fever (allergies to pollen), but goldenrods do not have airborne pollen.

**Comments:** As history has it, after the Boston Tea Party when settlers in Massachusetts protested British taxes by tossing bales of tea into Boston Harbor, the efforts to find a replacement for English tea resulted in the discovery of goldenrod tea, particularly from *Solidago odora*, which has a wide range in the United States as a species, with named varieties scattered throughout its range. The tea was known as "Liberty Tea" and became so popular it was exported to China where it commanded a high price under the name bouhea-tea. There are 21 goldenrod species in Florida, with 6 species divided into named varieties. All can be used for tea, but *Solidago odora* is the most documented species in the early literature. Native Americans used goldenrods medicinally to alleviate pain, counteract a love potion, treat cancer, spasms, and upset stomach, and as a gargle to relieve sore throats. An indigenous tribe in Canada even made a goldenrod wash to treat children who do not laugh.

**Uses:** The fully open flowers can be harvested, dried, and boiled to create, as German American botanist Frederick Pursh (1774–1820) wrote in 1807, "a most agreeable substitute for tea." Another way early settlers prepared tea from this goldenrod was to harvest the anise-scented leaves of var. *odora*, dry them over a slow fire, and then boil them in water. The leaf tea was praised as "having a good taste."

## COMMON SOWTHISTLE
*Sonchus oleraceus*

**Also called:** Annual sowthistle
**Nativity:** Introduced from Europe
**Florida range:** Throughout all of Florida
**Habitat:** Mostly disturbed sites, including residential landscapes
**Description:** Annual or biennial, often with hollow stems, with leaf blades variously shaped from oblong, obovate, or somewhat triangular, with lobed margins, reaching 10" long and 3" wide and becoming smaller up the stem. Flower heads are yellow and measure about ⅝" wide. Seeds are wind dispersed.
**Cautions:** Native Americans made an infusion from the plant and used it as an abortifacient, so women in early stages of pregnancy should avoid consuming this species. Wash the leaves thoroughly if harvesting from lawns or roadsides due to possible pollutants and pesticides.

**Comments:** This is a common weed of disturbed sites, including lawns and gardens. It is native to Europe but has traveled worldwide in tropical and temperate regions where it has become a source of food and herbal medicines. Native Americans in Arizona used the white latex to cure an opium habit, without medical proof that it was effective. The leaves are high in calcium, phosphorus, iron, and Vitamin A.

**Uses:** Young leaves can be picked and eaten raw or cooked as greens. The bitter taste of older leaves can be remedied by steaming or boiling. The roots can be dried, ground, and brewed as a coffee substitute.

## COMMON DANDELION
*Taraxacum officinale*

**Also called:** Kanphool (Eurasia)
**Nativity:** Introduced from Eurasia
**Florida range:** Scattered populations throughout much of Florida
**Habitat:** Mostly disturbed sites, including residential landscapes
**Description:** Herbaceous perennial to about 14" tall with horizontal or erect leaves that are shallowly to deeply lobed and range in shape from oblanceolate, oblong, or obovate, measuring 2"–16" long and up to 4" wide. Flower heads are yellow to orange-yellow, up to about 1½" wide with numerous ray florets.
**Cautions:** Some people have experienced dermatitis from contact with the milky sap. Avoid harvesting in areas where pesticides may have been used.
**Comments:** Common dandelion leaves are regarded as being very nutritious and are high in protein, carbohydrates, calcium, phosphorus, iron, potassium, Vitamin A, and many other vitamins.
**Uses:** Leaves can be eaten raw or cooked as a potherb. Younger leaves will be less bitter, as will leaves that are harvested in the winter months, though reportedly they contain lower concentrations of vitamins and minerals. The roots can also be eaten raw or cooked but are quite bitter. The flower buds can be pickled in vinegar and added to salads as a tasty treat. The leaves and roots have been used to flavor beer, and the roots of 2-year-old plants

can be harvested in the fall months, then dried and roasted to use as a pleasant-tasting, caffeine-free coffee substitute. The ray florets (or "petals") can be used to brew an herbal tea and to make dandelion wine. If you know where there are fields of dandelions, try the following wine recipe.

## RECIPE

**Dandelion Wine**

(12–13 percent alcohol)
3 quarts dandelion flower petals (do not use whole flowers or it will taste bitter)
1 gallon water
2 unpeeled oranges
1 unpeeled lemon (or lime)
3 pounds sugar (turbinado sugar is best)
1 package wine yeast
1 pound of raisins (or dried cranberries, sold as Craisins)

Dandelion wine

1. Place flower petals in a stainless-steel pot, crock, or ceramic bowl. Bring water to a boil in a separate pot and pour it over the flower petals.

2. Use a grater to zest about half of the orange and lemon (or lime) peel and use a sharp knife to remove the remaining peel, taking care to not include very much of the white pith below the peel. Cut away the white pith and slice the orange and lemon crossways into thin, round strips.

3. Add the zest to the water with the petals and bring to a boil. Add the sugar and stir until dissolved, then allow to cool.

4. Pour the contents through a strainer into a crock to remove the solids, then add the yeast, citrus slices, and raisins to the flower water.

5. Cover and allow to ferment for about 90 days while stirring daily with a wooden spoon for the first couple of weeks. Once fermented, pour contents through a strainer into a large bowl.

6. Fill sterilized bottles with the fermented liquid, then place a deflated balloon over the top of each bottle to check for further fermentation. When the balloons remain deflated for a day or two, fermentation is complete.

7. Cork the bottles and store in a cool, dark place for several months before serving.

## ORIENTAL FALSE HAWKSBEARD
*Youngia japonica*

**Also called:** Japanese sandal
**Nativity:** Introduced from Japan and China
**Florida range:** Throughout all of Florida
**Habitat:** Mostly disturbed sites, including residential landscapes
**Description:** This annual or biennial produces a rosette of elliptic or ovate leaves with rounded lobes, typically measuring about 3"–5" long and 1"–1½" wide. Flower heads are congested at the top of an erect stem, reaching 6"–12" tall.
**Cautions:** Wash the leaves thoroughly if harvesting from lawns or roadsides due to possible pesticides.
**Comments:** This pantropical species is one of the most common weeds in Florida, found throughout the state in vacant lots, lawns, gardens, roadsides, and even sidewalk cracks.
**Uses:** Tender young leaves can be steamed or boiled for 10 minutes and served as a side dish, or they can be eaten raw if you are out hiking. Young leaves have a mild flavor, but older leaves may be slightly bitter. Try sprinkling the cooked greens with cider vinegar before serving, or top with grated parmesan cheese. In China, the plant is used medicinally in a decoction to reduce inflammation and to treat boils and snakebites.

# BATACEAE (SALTWORT FAMILY)

## SALTWORT
*Batis maritima*

**Also called:** Beachwort, pickleweed, sea fennel
**Nativity:** Native
**Florida range:** Bay and Nassau Counties south along both coasts into the Florida Keys
**Habitat:** Salt marshes, mangroves, and other saline coastal habitats
**Description:** Herbaceous perennial with numerous spreading branches that root at the tip, forming extensive colonies. The succulent, linear leaves are opposite and average 1"–2" long. Ovoid-cylindric, axillary spikes bear tiny male and female flowers.
**Cautions:** The salty juice from the succulent leaves is irritating to the eyes, so avoid wiping your eyes if you've crushed the leaves with your fingers.
**Comments:** This species is often a dominant plant in salt marsh prairies and is a larval host plant of the great southern white and eastern pygmy blue butterflies. The branches become so entangled that they make walking through salt marsh habitat difficult.
**Uses:** The salty leaves are edible raw and can be picked and eaten or chopped and added to salads. The leaves can also be pickled in vinegar or cooked as a pre-salted potherb. The leaves are high in iodine and are eaten as a way to avoid goiter (enlargement of the thyroid gland).

# BORAGINACEAE (BORAGE FAMILY)

## CHIGGERY GRAPES
*Heliotropium verdcourtii (*formerly *Tournefortia hirsutissima)*

**Also called:** Hog hook (Jamaica)
**Nativity:** Native
**Florida range:** Vouchered from Hendry, Collier, Miami-Dade, and Monroe (both mainland and Keys) Counties
**Habitat:** Hammocks
**Description:** This is a high-climbing woody vine with stiff hairs covering the leaves and stems. Alternate, elliptic to ovate, scabrous leaves measure up to 8" long and 4" wide. Fragrant, white flowers are produced in branching cymes, with each flower measuring about ¼" wide, and are followed by white, opaque, oval fruits to about ⅜" across.
**Cautions:** The hairs on the leaves can cause skin irritation on sensitive people. If you own horses, do not grow any members of the genus *Heliotropium* because the leaves can cause severe liver damage, and symptoms of poisoning reportedly may not appear for up to 8 months after ingestion.

**Comments:** This state-listed endangered species can become a woody liana in hammocks, with a stout trunk to 5" in diameter that reaches high into the tree canopy. In cultivation it can be grown on a stout fence or allowed to climb into the canopy of large trees. When flowering in early spring, the flowers are swarmed by butterflies, and birds feast on the fruits. The common name comes from the practice of rubbing crushed leaves on the skin as a remedy for chigger bites.

**Uses:** The fruits can be picked and eaten, but, if foraging in the wild, be certain to spit the seeds of this endangered species out so they will have a chance to germinate. It is noted in books on bush medicine that the leaves and roots are commonly used in the Caribbean islands to brew medicinal teas or decoctions used to treat skin diseases, venereal disease, Type 2 diabetes, hypertension, jaundice, vomiting, and as a wash for women to use after giving birth.

# BRASSICACEAE (MUSTARD FAMILY)

## COASTAL SEAROCKET
*Cakile lanceolata*

**Also called:** Pork bush (Bahamas)
**Nativity:** Native
**Florida range:** Along both coasts of Florida into the Florida Keys
**Habitat:** Beach dunes and coastal shorelines
**Description:** Annual or short-lived perennial with much-branched, erect or sprawling stems. Leaves are pinnately lobed or ovate to ovate-lanceolate, with smooth margins. Flowers have 4 white petals (rarely lavender), green at the base.
**Cautions:** Juice from the stems and leaves can irritate the eyes.
**Comments:** Another species, *Cakile edentula* subsp. *harperi* (American searocket), occurs along the east coast of Florida from Nassau County south to St. Lucie County. *Flora of North*

*America* recognizes a third species, *Cakile constricta*, in Florida, and divides *Cakile lanceolata* into 3 separate subspecies, with subsp. *fusiformis* occurring in Florida. Coastal searocket is the namesake of the Florida Native Plant Society's Sea Rocket Chapter, appropriately located in Brevard County where rockets are fired from Cape Canaveral.

**Uses:** Tender new leaves and shoots can be picked and eaten raw or steamed as a vegetable side dish. Older leaves can be boiled as a potherb. The leaves have been described as having a radish-like flavor, and some plants produce leaves that have a distinct bite to them, so much so that they have been used as a replacement for wasabi in Japanese cuisine. In the Caribbean the leaves are boiled and placed on persistent sores as a cleansing agent. In the Bahamas the leaves are cooked with pork.

## VIRGINA PEPPERWEED
*Lepidium virginicum*

**Also called:** Peppergrass, Virginian peppergrass, wild peppergrass
**Nativity:** Native
**Florida range:** Throughout all of Florida
**Habitat:** Mostly disturbed sites, including residential landscapes, roadsides, and canal banks
**Description:** Annual with erect stems averaging 10"–20" tall, lined with linear-lanceolate stem leaves averaging 1"–2" long and ⅛"–¼" wide. Basal leaves are longer and wider, withering at anthesis (flowering). The flat, oval seed capsules (pedicels) line the stems and typically cant upward. Minuscule, white flowers are in racemes at the top of the stems.

**Cautions:** The juice from crushed stems or leaves can burn the eyes.

**Comments:** This is a ubiquitous weed throughout Florida but is a larval host plant of the checkered white, great southern white, and cabbage white butterflies, so it is a weed worth tolerating.

**Uses:** The flat, immature seed capsules can be picked and eaten and have a distinct peppery taste. The seed capsules and the mustard-tasting young leaves can be added to salads for a little extra flavor and zing, as well as to vegetable dishes in lieu of black pepper. Also, seeds can be planted and the seedlings harvested and eaten as a spring salad. Eaten fresh, the leaves allegedly have a detoxifying effect on the body. Native Americans brewed a leaf tea to treat poison ivy rash, and the tea is regarded as having many medicinal benefits, such as to treat scurvy (Vitamin C deficiency), diabetes, and to expel hookworms and tapeworms in the intestines.

# CACTACEAE (CACTUS FAMILY)

## FLORIDA PRICKLY PEAR
*Opuntia austrina (*formerly referred to as *Opuntia humifusa)*

**Also called:** Devil's tongue
**Nativity:** Native
**Florida range:** Endemic to peninsular Florida (absent from the Florida Panhandle and the Florida Keys)
**Habitat:** Pinelands, sandhills, scrub, coastal dunes, and other open, sandy habitats
**Description:** Low-growing cactus with round or oblong, succulent pads (cladodes). The pads average 3"–5" long and 2"–3" wide and bear wickedly sharp spines that range ½"–2" long, often clustered. Very showy yellow to yellowish-orange flowers reach about 2½" wide, followed by cone-shaped, red to reddish-purple, 1"–2" fruits (berries).
**Cautions:** The sharp spines can cause painful puncture wounds. Tiny, but extremely irritating hairlike spines (called glochids) are produced at the areoles or surrounding the base of the main spines. The glochids are usually barbed and easily detach and lodge in the skin, causing intense irritation. Pull them out with tweezers or try placing duct tape over them and then pulling it off.

**Comments:** There are 5 other native *Opuntia* species in Florida (or 6 if *Opuntia keyensis* is included as a valid species) along with 3 introduced, non-native species naturalized in the state. Both *Opuntia abjecta* and *Opuntia ochrocentra* are endemic to the Florida Keys. The cactus commonly eaten in Mexico is *Opuntia cochinillifera*, or cochineal cactus. The pads are skinned, boiled, or fried and are called *nopales*. It is naturalized in central and southern Florida, mostly from people discarding pieces of the cactus, which then take root. You can find pads for sale in grocery stores near Mexican American populations.

**Uses:** Ripe fruits can be peeled and eaten fresh. The pads can be very carefully peeled with a sharp kitchen knife, but first snip off the long spines and wear gloves to avoid the small glochids (see Cautions). Wash and then dice the peeled pads into 1" squares, cover with water in a stainless-steel pot, and boil over medium heat for about 10 minutes or until tender. Rinse. They can be eaten as is or gently sautéed with garlic, butter, and herbs. They can also be diced into smaller pieces and added to tacos. All prickly pear cactus species can be prepared in this manner, but note that the small *Opuntia abjecta* in the Florida Keys is a state-listed endangered species and the large *Opuntia stricta* of the Florida mainland and Keys is a state-listed threatened species.

## RECIPE

### Prickly Pear Fruit Vinaigrette

Prickly pear fruits

4 ripe cactus fruits, peeled and washed
1 banana, peeled
4 tablespoons honey
2–4 tablespoons red wine vinegar
Juice from 2 limes or 2 lemons (or 1 of each)

1. Carefully peel the cactus fruits to ensure that all the small spines, called glochids, are completely removed, then wash them under a faucet to be doubly certain.

2. Place the peeled and washed cactus fruits and the banana in a blender along with the rest of the ingredients and blend until smooth. For tarter flavor, add more vinegar; for sweeter, add more honey.

3. Strain to remove the seeds if you like. Use as a salad dressing or to flavor cooked greens.

# CARICACEAE (PAPAYA FAMILY)

## PAPAYA
*Carica papaya*

**Also called:** Pawpaw (although that name is most often used for plants in the genus *Asimina*), *fruta bomba* in Spanish-speaking countries

**Nativity:** Considered native to Florida based on seeds unearthed in a Calusa midden in Lee County that archaeologists dated to AD 300

**Florida range:** St. Johns, Putnam, and Hernando Counties south through mainland Florida into the Florida Keys

**Habitat:** Hammock margins, canopy gaps, and disturbed sites

**Description:** Single-trunked, non-woody, tree-like plant with deeply incised leaf blades ranging 12"–18" wide on long petioles. The leaves are crowded at the top of the trunk, and male and female flowers are borne on separate plants. The small, yellow, male flowers are on long, branched spikes, with each flower measuring about ¾" across. Female flowers are solitary and produced close to the trunk, each measuring about 2" wide. The fruits on wild native forms of papaya are only about 2½" wide, or about the size of a tennis ball. There are, however, occasional cultivated forms that have escaped into natural areas in southern and central Florida, and these produce much larger fruits.

**Uses:** The ripe fruits of papaya can be peeled with a knife or potato peeler and eaten raw, and are regarded as one of the healthiest fruits you can eat. The fruits of the native form, however, pale in comparison to the improved, much larger, cultivated varieties. Unripe, green papaya fruits can be peeled, sliced, and cooked as a vegetable. Also, papaya sap from the green, unripe fruits contains papain, an enzyme that breaks down proteins and is used as an ingredient in meat tenderizer. In lieu of purchasing commercial meat tenderizer, simply slit the skin of unripe papaya fruits and apply the white, milky sap to tough meats. Leave it on the meat overnight. In supplement form, papain is used to ease the pain of a sore throat, aid digestion, help heal wounds, ease sore muscles, and treat symptoms of shingles. For the following recipe you will need a larger, cultivated papaya fruit or up to 10 wild papaya fruits.

## RECIPE

**Papaya Smoothie**

1 medium-sized papaya or 8–10 small, wild papaya fruits
½ cup milk
3 tablespoons fresh lime juice
½ tablespoon lime zest (shaved lime peel)
¼ cup honey (or sugar)
½ teaspoon vanilla extract
1 cup crushed ice

Peel and deseed the papaya and cut into cubes. Add the papaya and all the other ingredients in a blender and blend on high for 20–30 seconds. Pour into a glass and enjoy.

# CELASTRACEAE (STAFFTREE FAMILY)

## QUAILBERRY
*Crossopetalum ilicifolium*

**Also called:** Ground holly, Christmas berry
**Nativity:** Native
**Florida range:** Collier and Miami-Dade Counties and the Monroe County Keys
**Habitat:** Pinelands
**Description:** Somewhat woody perennial with prostrate or ascending branches and mostly opposite, ovate to elliptic, holly-like toothed leaves averaging ½" long and slightly narrower. The tiny flower petals are red and are followed by bright red, ¼" fruits.
**Cautions:** Some members of this family are known to contain terpenes that can cause allergic reactions in some people, but that is not known to be true for this genus.
**Comments:** This low-growing species would make an excellent border plant or even a groundcover for sunny locations in the landscape. Numerous birds feast on the fruits, including quail. A decoction is made from the roots in the West Indies to treat kidney stones and other issues with the kidneys.
**Uses:** The ripe fruits can be picked and eaten, but in my opinion they would be survival food at best.

## MAIDENBERRY
*Crossopetalum rhacoma*

**Also called:** Rhacoma, Christmas berry

**Nativity:** Native

**Florida range:** Sarasota and Miami-Dade Counties into the Monroe County Keys. Dr. Dan Austin (1943–2015), in his book *Florida Ethnobotany*, stated that this species historically occurred in Broward, Palm Beach, Collier, and Lee Counties, but there are no herbarium specimens to support that claim.

**Habitat:** Rocky shorelines, hammock margins, and coastal swales

**Description:** Woody shrub or small tree to 10' tall but usually half that height. Angular branches bear opposite, ½"–1", linear-lanceolate to obovate leaves with crenulate margins. Tiny flowers are tinged with red and clustered in the leaf axils. The fruits ripen red and are about ¼" wide.

**Cautions:** This is a state-listed threatened species so, when sampling fruits where it is legal to forage, plant the seeds to help produce more plants, and leave plenty of fruits for the birds. A better option is to purchase plants from nurseries in South Florida that specialize in Florida native plants and harvest the seeds from your own landscape. Resident and migrant birds in your neighborhood will appreciate the fruits, too.

**Comments:** The fruits of this species are pleasantly sweet, but there's very little to eat around the seed.

**Uses:** Ripe, red fruits can be picked and eaten fresh. Decoctions from the roots and leaves have been used in bush medicine to treat bladder and kidney infections.

# FLORIDA BOXWOOD
*Schaefferia frutescens*

**Also called:** Yellowwood (this name is also used for *Zanthoxylum flavum*, native to the Florida Keys)

**Nativity:** Native

**Florida range:** Miami-Dade County and the Monroe County Keys

**Habitat:** Tropical hardwood hammocks

**Description:** Dioecious woody shrub or small tree to 16' tall or more with alternate, elliptic to lanceolate leaves averaging 1"–2" long and ⅝"–⅞" wide. Flowers are produced along the stems and measure about ³⁄₁₆" across. Small, round fruits reach about ¼" wide, ripening orange to red.

**Comments:** This state-listed endangered species is little known outside the southernmost counties in Florida. It is uncommon in the hammocks and coastal strand of the Florida Keys but can be found in select southern Florida nurseries that specialize in native plants. The fruits are quite small and unremarkable in flavor, but the species is included here due to its use in the Greater Antilles.

**Uses:** The fruits can be picked and eaten fresh but are not very flavorful. In Cuba the fruits are sold in street markets as an aphrodisiac, without any medical proof that it works. A leaf tea is brewed in Haiti to treat influenza and coughs.

# CHENOPODIACEAE (GOOSEFOOT FAMILY)

## CRESTED SALTBUSH
*Atriplex pentandra (*formerly *Atriplex arenaria)*

**Also called:** Seashore orach, pretty woman, good woman, broth-of-the-sea
**Nativity:** Native
**Florida range:** Coastal counties statewide
**Habitat:** Coastal dunes, rocky shorelines, and salt marshes
**Description:** Herbaceous perennial with angled stems (often red) with broadly obovate or rhombic-ovate leaves averaging 1"–1½" long and ⅜"–½" wide, typically with wavy margins. Male flowers are in dense terminal spikes, and female flowers are clustered in the leaf axils.
**Cautions:** The salty juice from the leaves can irritate the eyes.
**Comments:** Crested saltbush can be locally common along beaches, salt flats, and saline marshes from the Florida Panhandle south along both coasts through the Florida Keys. Some taxonomists place this genus in the Amaranth family (Amaranthaceae).
**Uses:** The salty leaves can be boiled as greens or added to stews and soups. The leaves are used in the Caribbean to make a salty broth used in cooking, and can also be boiled with meats to add saltiness.

## LAMB'S QUARTERS
*Chenopodium album* var. *missouriensis*

**Also called:** White goosefoot, pigweed
**Nativity:** This narrow-leaved variety is considered to be native to Florida in *Flora of the Southeastern United States* (Weakley et al., 2022).
**Florida range:** Throughout most all of Florida, from the Panhandle to the Florida Keys
**Habitat:** Mostly disturbed sites but especially agricultural fields and roadsides that border agricultural fields
**Description:** Annual, herbaceous species reaching 12"–48" tall or more with angled stems and alternate, mostly lanceolate upper leaves. Tiny, white or green flowers appear in axillary and terminal racemes. A single plant may produce as many as 30,000 to 75,000 small, black seeds.
**Cautions:** Some plants in this family are high in oxalates, so they should not be consumed regularly or in large quantities, especially for those who are prone to kidney stones or other kidney issues.

**Comments:** The name lamb's quarters is thought to come from the name of the British harvest festival called Lammas Quarter. This festival was associated both with sacrificial lambs and with the *Chenopodium album* that they cooked with lamb during the festival. The taxonomy of this species is extremely confusing and complex. Many taxonomists simply call it *Chenopodium album* and let it go at that. The *Florida Plant Atlas* places it in the Amaranth family (Amaranthaceae), while *Flora of North America* and *Flora of the Southeastern United States* keep it in the Goosefoot family (Chenopodiaceae); *Flora of North America* also states that it is one of the worst weeds on the planet. But they cite another species called *Chenopodium missouriensis* as a "confusing taxon" that "appears to be a native form of *Chenopodium album*." Then they go on to state that it flowers in mid-September regardless of when it germinated, and that it occurs in the United States in the central low-lands and part of the Appalachian plateau. And finally, in the recently published *Flora of the Southeastern United States* (Weakley et al., 2022), the plant photographed keys out to what is referred to as *Chenopodium album* var. *missouriensis*, based on the lanceolate upper leaves and branching habit. *Chenopodium album* var. *album* has wide, ovate to rhombic leaves with coarsely toothed margins.

**Uses:** The tender young leaves can be picked and eaten or added to salads. Older leaves can be boiled or steamed as you would other greens and served as a side dish. The seeds can be germinated on a wet paper towel and served as sprouts, or the seeds can be ground into a form of flour to use as a nutritional thickener for gravy, stews, or soup. If you harvest plants from fallow farm fields, be certain to wash them thoroughly to avoid any residual chemicals sprayed on commercial crops.

# PERENNIAL GLASSWORT
*Salicornia ambigua*

**Also called:** Virginia glasswort, pickleweed
**Nativity:** Native
**Florida range:** Coastal counties throughout Florida into the Florida Keys
**Habitat:** Saline coastal habitats
**Description:** Herbaceous perennial forming extensive colonies by underground rhizomes. The branches are formed of fleshy joints that are mostly erect along the main, horizontal stem, with leaves reduced to minute scales. Minuscule, white flowers appear on the upper jointed stems.
**Cautions:** The salty juice from the leaves can irritate the eyes.
**Comments:** Another Florida native species is annual glasswort (*Salicornia bigelovii*). Other species are native to Europe and Asia and are widely cooked and eaten. Some taxonomists place this genus in the Amaranth family (Amaranthaceae).
**Uses:** The leaves can be eaten fresh as a salty snack or added to salads, soups, or stews. The leaves can also be pickled in vinegar. If cooked as a potherb, it is best to soak the leaves in water overnight prior to cooking to help reduce the saltiness.

## SEA BLITE
*Suaeda linearis*

**Also called:** Annual seepweed

**Nativity:** Native

**Florida range:** Coastal counties along the west coast of Florida from the central Panhandle south to mainland Monroe County and along the entire eastern peninsula south into the Florida Keys

**Habitat:** Coastal dunes, salt marshes, mangrove forests, and rocky shorelines

**Description:** Herbaceous perennial (annual in cold temperate regions), 10"–30" tall, with green or red stems and green or red, narrowly linear leaves 1"–2" long. Bisexual flowers are usually densely arranged on branched spikes.

**Cautions:** Salt marsh habitat is also home to eastern diamondback rattlesnakes, so step with due caution.

**Comments:** Sea blite can be a common species in salt marsh habitat where it grows in the company of saltwort (*Batis maritima*), glasswort (*Salicornia* spp.), and other salt-tolerant species. It can also be found along trails that bisect mangrove/buttonwood forests, especially in the southern counties. Some taxonomists place this genus in the Amaranth family (Amaranthaceae).

Uses: The leaves can be picked and eaten as a salty snack, added to salads, or used as an ingredient in stews, soups, and other dishes in lieu of salt. You can also soak the leaves in cold water overnight to remove some of the saltiness and boil them as a side dish. The following recipe comes from the mother of a Bahamian friend in Miami.

## RECIPE

**Bahamian Chicken Soup**

2 quarts water
2 skinned and boned chicken breasts
8 ounces unsalted chicken broth
1 cup chopped sea blite leaves
4 small white potatoes, chopped
½ cup shredded carrots
2 celery stalks with leaves, chopped
1 jalapeño pepper, seeded and diced (optional)
1 medium-sized leek, chopped (substitute with scallions if leeks aren't available)
1 clove garlic, smashed and chopped
1 teaspoon rosemary
Chopped cilantro leaves
Grated parmesan or Romano cheese

1. Add the water and chicken broth to a large pot and bring to a boil.

2. Cut the chicken into chunks and add to the pot, then boil for 30 minutes.

3. Add all the other ingredients except the cilantro and cheese and cook over medium heat for 30–45 minutes.

4. Scoop into serving bowls and sprinkle with grated cheese and chopped cilantro leaves. Serve and enjoy.

# CHRYSOBALANACEAE (COCOPLUM FAMILY)

Purple-fruited form    White-fruited form    Pink-fruited form

## COCOPLUM
*Chrysobalanus icaco*

**Also called:** Paradise plum, icaco

**Nativity:** Native

**Florida range:** Brevard and Pasco Counties south along both coasts and across all of Florida south of Lake Okeechobee, including the Florida Keys

**Habitat:** Pinelands, hammock margins, coastal strand, dunes, wooded swamps, and sloughs

**Description:** Spreading shrub or tree to about 20' tall with alternate, broadly elliptic to nearly oval leaves 1"–2" long and wide. The 5-lobed flowers are about ¼" wide, followed by purple, pink, or white oval fruits averaging ¾"–1" wide.

**Cautions:** Tea from the leaves may cause hypoglycemia (low blood sugar), which may be useful for people suffering from high blood sugar levels.

**Comments:** Purple-fruited plants bear fruits that are oblong in shape, while white or pink-ish fruits on coastal plants are larger and more rounded. The new growth on purple-fruited plants is red, while on white-fruited forms it is pale green.

**Uses:** Eaten out of hand the fruits have a pleasant, somewhat subtle flavor with a marshmallow-like texture. The kernel inside the seed is edible and has an almond-like fla-vor. To harvest the kernels, simply crack open the outer seed coat as you would a nut. The seeds are high in oil content and can be dried, strung on sticks, and burned like candles. The fruit pulp has long been used to make cocoplum jam; simply boil the fruit pulp in water with sugar and lemon juice until thickened. Pectin is not needed if you boil the mixture slowly until it thickens naturally. It will keep for several weeks in the refrigerator. Follow the direc-tions for any jam recipe.

# GOPHER APPLE
*Geobalanus oblongifolius (*some taxonomists favor *Licania michauxii* as the "correct" name*)*

**Also called:** Ground oak
**Nativity:** Native
**Florida range:** Throughout all of Florida
**Habitat:** Pinelands, scrub, sandhills, coastal strand, and roadsides
**Description:** Rhizomatous shrub forming spreading colonies with individual plants typically reaching less than 10" tall, especially in pinelands where they are burned to the ground by fire. Leaves are oblanceolate to narrowly oblong, averaging 2"–3" long and ¾"–1" wide. Flowers are white, measuring about ¼" across with triangular sepals. Fruits are about 1" long and ¾" wide, ripening white to pink.
**Cautions:** Tea from the leaves may cause hypoglycemia (low blood sugar), which may be useful for people suffering from high blood sugar levels.
**Comments:** The common name relates to the fruits being produced at eye level to a gopher tortoise, which commonly feeds on them.
**Uses:** Ripe fruits can be picked and eaten and are similar in taste and texture to the related cocoplum (*Chrysobalanus icaco*), described previously. An herbal tea can be brewed from fresh or dried leaves.

# CLUSIACEAE (MANGOSTEEN FAMILY)

## COASTAL PLAIN ST. JOHN'S-WORT
*Hypericum brachyphyllum*

**Also called:** Shortleaf St. John's-wort
**Nativity:** Native
**Florida range:** Throughout most all of mainland Florida (absent from the Florida Keys)
**Habitat:** Pine flatwoods, coastal plains, pond margins, and depressions
**Description:** Woody, evergreen shrub 2'–4' tall, forming rounded mounds of leaves and with reddish-brown, exfoliating bark. The opposite leaves are linear, glabrous, with revolute margins, averaging ¼"–½" long. Flowers measure about ½" across with 5 yellow petals. Fruits are cylindrical capsules.
**Cautions:** St. John's-wort taken in capsule form can cause increased sensitivity to sunlight and, in large doses, can cause dizziness, anxiety, fatigue, headache, or sexual dysfunction. It is taken to treat mild depression, but there are warnings to not take it when pregnant or breast-feeding, and it may also weaken the effectiveness of birth control pills, HIV drugs, and cancer medications, so consult your physician before taking capsules. Tea made from the flowers can also cause photosensitivity, so it is wise to avoid sitting in the sun after consuming the tea to avoid skin burns, especially if you are fair-skinned.

**Comments:** There are 34 native *Hypericum* species in Florida, so foragers will likely encounter one or more species in their travels around the state. Coastal plain St. John's-wort is one of the more common species. Most species are low shrubs, while *Hypericum lissophloeus* of the central Panhandle reaches 8' tall or more.

**Uses:** The fresh flowers of all species are edible and sometimes used as a decorative garnish in salads, plus the leaves and flowers are used to brew an herbal tea, but the tea takes time for some people to get used to due to the bitter and astringent taste. Once you've become accustomed to the taste, you will likely find the tea to be quite agreeable. Add honey, sugar, or lemon to taste. St. John's-wort tea is also effectively used as a wash to treat burns, insect bites, sunburn, and small wounds. *Hypericum* species have a long history of medicinal uses by Native Americans and settlers to treat depression, viruses, coughs, menstrual cramps, and as a sedative to calm the nerves and induce restful sleep.

# CONVOLVULACEAE (MORNING-GLORY FAMILY)

## MOONFLOWER
*Ipomoea alba*

**Also called:** Moonvine, tropical white morning-glory
**Nativity:** Native
**Florida range:** Duval and Levy Counties south through mainland Florida into the Florida Keys
**Habitat:** Hammock margins, coastal strand, and fencerows
**Description:** A high-climbing, aggressive vine with heart-shaped leaves averaging 4"–5" long and 3"–3½" wide. White, fragrant, nocturnal flowers reach 3½"–4" across, closing by mid-morning.
**Cautions:** The very toxic *Datura wrightii* is a non-native, unrelated species that is also called moonflower, so let this be a reminder to never use common names as a means of identification. The seeds of some morning-glories contain lysergic acid amines and can cause delusion and hallucinations.
**Comments:** This is a common vine within its range in Florida and is most visible along roadsides early in the morning before the flowers have closed. The flowers open at night and attract sphinx moths as pollinators.
**Uses:** The tender new growth and immature flower buds can be picked and eaten raw or steamed and served as a side dish.

# MAN-OF-THE-EARTH
*Ipomoea pandurata*

**Also called:** Wild potato vine, man root, Indian potato
**Nativity:** Native
**Florida range:** Throughout northern and central Florida south to Collier, Highlands, and St. Lucie Counties
**Habitat:** Forest margins, edges of streams, thickets, and disturbed sites
**Description:** The stems of this vine may reach 30' long with fiddle-shaped (pandurate) or heart-shaped leaves that measure 4"–6" long and 2½"–3½" wide. The flowers are white with a purplish throat and average about 3" wide.
**Cautions:** Large, older roots are bitter and inedible.
**Comments:** The common names relate to the large, underground tuberous root produced by the plant. When cooked, the root tastes somewhat like the related sweet potato (*Ipomoea batatas*). Harvest from private property with the landowner's permission, or grow your own from harvested seed or from plants purchased in nurseries that specialize in Florida native plants. Harvesting the root kills the plant, so harvesting roots of wild plants in preserves where foraging is allowed is unethical.
**Uses:** The underground root can be washed and baked, much like a sweet potato, but older roots may weigh 20 pounds or more and will taste bitter, so look for younger roots that are about the size of a sweet potato. Cook in a microwave for 6–7 minutes or bake in a conventional oven at 350ºF for 30–45 minutes, or until tender. Serve as you would a sweet potato.

## RAILROAD VINE
*Ipomoea pes-caprae*

**Also called:** Bay hops, goat's foot, seaside yam (Bahamas)
**Nativity:** Native
**Florida range:** Coastal counties throughout most all of Florida south into the Florida Keys
**Habitat:** Beach dunes
**Description:** Trailing herbaceous vine with rounded, 2"–4" leaves that are notched at the tip. The stems can reach 20' long or more and are an important beach dune stabilizer. The pinkish-purple, funnel-shaped flowers are about 3" wide with darker rose-purple nectar guides radiating out from the throat.
**Cautions:** Small amounts of ergot alkaloids have reportedly been found in the seeds. If eaten in sufficient quantity, ergot can cause strange hallucinations, a feeling of itchy and burning skin, gangrene, and even death. It was ergot poisoning from infected grain that caused Puritans in Salem, Massachusetts, to believe that those who were infected with it were witches, and after being tried in court, they were summarily burned at the stake.
**Comments:** This species helps stabilize beach dunes from wind and wave action and is often cultivated for beach dune restoration projects. The name railroad vine alludes to its long stems that often grow parallel to each other down the beach, like railroad tracks. It is used in the Bahamas to treat swelling caused by an injury or arthritis.
**Uses:** To treat swelling, muscle aches, or arthritis pain, prepare a poultice by bruising several leaves with a mallet or rock, then add salt to the leaves and apply them like a poultice to the affected area. Crushed leaves have also been used to launder clothes when detergents are unavailable.

# CUCURBITACEAE (GOURD FAMILY)

## SEMINOLE PUMPKIN
*Cucurbita moschata*

**Also called:** Seminole gourd, winter crookneck squash

**Nativity:** Introduced from the tropical Americas long before European contact

**Florida range:** Vouchered from Escambia, Leon, Hillsborough, and Miami-Dade Counties but cultivated in many other counties

**Habitat:** Disturbed sites

**Description:** Trailing vine with long stems bearing rounded, coarsely toothed leaves measuring 6"–8" long and wide. Yellow flowers average about 3½" wide, opening in the morning and closing by midday.

**Cautions:** Avoid mistaking this species for the native, but inedible, Okeechobee gourd (*Cucurbita okeechobeensis*), which is round, mottled green, and slightly larger than a baseball.

**Comments:** This species has a long history as a staple food among Native Americans, including the Hopi, Iroquois, Maricopa, Navajo, and Seminole.

Uses: The Seminole pumpkin can be boiled, baked, or microwaved whole, in halves, or cut into chunks. Treat it like you would acorn or butternut squash by adding butter, ground cinnamon, or nutmeg before serving. Other options include Seminole pumpkin soup (see recipe) or cutting the pumpkin into strips and either frying them in oil or sun-drying for future use. The seeds can be dried, parched, shelled, and eaten as a snack or added to salads. The young shoots on the vine can be cooked as a potherb, and the flowers can be cooked and eaten. Dr. Julia Morton (1912–1996) wrote that the flowers are popular in Italy, Greece, and Turkey, where they add them to sandwiches or bake them after being stuffed with meat and rice. Seeds of this species are available on the internet.

## RECIPE

**Seminole Pumpkin Soup**

3 pounds Seminole pumpkin
1 medium yellow onion
2 tablespoons extra-virgin olive oil
2 cloves garlic
2 tablespoons each fresh sage and rosemary
2 tablespoons fresh ginger
8 ounces vegetable broth
Salt
Chopped parsley or cilantro

1. Cut the pumpkin in half with a sharp knife, scoop out the seeds, slice off the skin, then dice the pumpkin into small cubes.

2. Peel and chop the onion. Sauté the onion in olive oil until it becomes translucent, then add the pumpkin cubes and cook until they begin to soften.

3. Smash the garlic cloves, then peel and chop. Chop the sage, rosemary, and ginger.

4. Stir the garlic, ginger, and herbs into the pumpkin mix, add the vegetable broth and simmer for 20 minutes, or until the pumpkin becomes soft. Add salt to taste.

5. Pour into a blender and blend on medium speed until the soup is silky smooth.

6. Pour into bowls and garnish with chopped parsley or cilantro.

## CREEPING CUCUMBER
*Melothria pendula*

**Also called:** Purging cherry (Brazil), mouse's melon (Belize)
**Nativity:** Native
**Florida range:** Throughout all of Florida
**Habitat:** Mostly disturbed sites such as fencerows, vacant lots, and residential landscapes
**Description:** The lobed leaves of this vine range 1"–1½" long and wide. Male and female yellow flowers are produced separately on the same plant and average ½" wide. The fruits are about ½"–⅜" long and, when green, resemble miniature watermelons. The fruits ripen black.
**Cautions:** Eating ripe (black) fruits may result in explosive diarrhea, so don't say you weren't warned!
**Comments:** In the literature there are references to the fruits being somewhat toxic, but they are widely consumed throughout the Bahamas, Caribbean, and Central America where they are sold in street markets. It is weedy in cultivation because birds eat the fruits and disperse the seeds.
**Uses:** The green, unripe fruits can be eaten fresh, chopped and added to salads, or pickled in vinegar.

# CYPERACEAE (SEDGE FAMILY)

## SAWGRASS
*Cladium jamaicense*

**Also called:** Jamaica swamp sawgrass
**Nativity:** Native
**Florida range:** Throughout most all of Florida, including the Florida Keys
**Habitat:** Short- and long-hydroperiod glades, pine rocklands, and freshwater marshes, often forming a monoculture
**Description:** A coarse sedge that may reach 6'–7' tall with flat to V-shaped leaves averaging 3'–4' long and up to about ½" wide, with margins lined with small, sharp, sawlike teeth. The inflorescence stands well above the leaves and bears brown flowers.
**Cautions:** Saw-like teeth along the leaf margins can slice through bare skin and leave painful cuts. If you plan to hike through sawgrass, wear long pants and a long-sleeved shirt.

**Comments:** Despite the common name, sawgrass is actually a sedge, not a grass. The vast sawgrass prairies of the Everglades are quite a sight, covering thousands of acres far beyond what the eye can see. It is a larval host plant of the Palatka skipper butterfly.

**Uses:** Although it may be painful to harvest due to the numerous sharp teeth on the leaf margins, the apical meristem, or "growing heart," on the plant is edible and tastes much like heart of palm. To harvest it, cut the plant off near the base and begin removing leaves until you reach the tender new growth in the center. The plant will later resprout and grow new leaves, exactly like what happens after fire burns the plant to the ground.

# EBENACEAE (PERSIMMON FAMILY)

## COMMON PERSIMMON
*Diospyros virginiana*

**Also called:** Virginia persimmon, possumwood
**Nativity:** Native
**Florida range:** Throughout all of Florida except the Florida Keys
**Habitat:** Hardwood forests, coastal strand, seasonally flooded woodlands, and strand swamps
**Description:** This is a dioecious, deciduous tree with dark green, glossy, broadly ovate to elliptic leaves that are typically smooth but may be slightly pubescent when young, averaging 3"–5" long and 1"–3" wide, with a pointed tip. Small flowers are solitary (female) or in clusters of 2 or 3 (male) and appear on branches of the current season. Fruits on female trees are produced from August to December and ripen orange to dark orange, each averaging 1"–2" wide.
**Cautions:** The unripe fruits are very astringent, and, if consumed, they may create a blockage in the upper intestines and require surgical removal.
**Comments:** If you decide to grow this tree in your landscape, remember that you will need both male and female trees, so it is best to purchase trees of flowering age so you can determine their sex. Male flowers have stamens and female flowers have pistils, if you recall your

high school biology. If you plan to grow trees from seed, when they are old enough to be placed in the ground you should plant at least 4 trees for the best chance of having at least 1 female tree. Another option is to air-layer branches off a known male and female tree.

**Uses:** Fully ripe fruits are delicious eaten fresh but are also used in pudding, smoothies, cakes, jams, cookies, and fruit salads. Fully ripe fruits can be found on the ground beneath female trees, but mature, unripe fruits can be picked and allowed to ripen at home. If eaten slightly unripe, the fruits are very astringent and will leave your mouth unpleasantly dry and chalky.

## RECIPE

**Persimmon Fruit Pudding**

2 cups persimmon pulp (skinned with seeds removed)
½ teaspoon baking soda
2 cups granulated sugar
2 eggs, beaten
2 cups all-purpose or whole wheat flour
2 teaspoons baking powder
½ teaspoon ground cinnamon
¼ teaspoon vanilla extract
2½ cups low-fat milk
4 tablespoons melted butter or margarine

1. Preheat oven to 325°F. Grease a 9-by-13-inch baking dish.

2. In a mixing bowl, combine persimmon pulp, baking soda, sugar, and beaten eggs. Mix well. Add flour, baking powder, cinnamon, vanilla, milk, and melted butter. Mix well.

3. Pour mixture into the greased baking dish and bake for 1 hour.

4. Remove from oven and let cool (the pudding will thicken as it cools).

# ERICACEAE (HEATH FAMILY)

## BLUE HUCKLEBERRY
*Gaylussacia frondosa*

**Also called:** Dangleberry

**Nativity:** Native

**Florida range:** Throughout the Panhandle and the northern peninsula south to Sarasota, Hardee, and Highlands Counties

**Habitat:** Forest margins, edges of wetlands, woodlands, meadows, and fields

**Description:** Rhizomatous shrub to about 6' tall with pubescent, gland-dotted, lanceolate leaves averaging 2"–2½" long and ½"–1" wide, often with brown pubescence below. Somewhat bell-shaped, white to pinkish flowers are produced in clusters, followed by oval, blueberry-size fruits that turn blue when ripe.

**Cautions:** Bears love to feast on huckleberries, so keep your wits about you when in bear country, and bring pepper spray.

**Comments:** Blue huckleberry forms rhizomatous thickets that provide cover for small mammals and birds, especially quail. Wild turkeys, bears, raccoons, and other wildlife eat the fruits. Look for it in well-drained, sandy soils of pine flatwoods, sandhills, and scrub, often near freshwater wetlands. The taxonomy of this species is confusing, with *Flora of North America* showing it ranging south to eastern Georgia, while *Flora of Florida* shows it ranging into south-central Florida. This is apparently due to *Flora of North America* recognizing two other entities, *Gaylussacia nana* and *Gaylussacia tomentosa*, which are shown ranging into Florida. So it depends on whether you're a taxonomic lumper or splitter as to what is represented in Florida. In this book I am following *Flora of Florida* to keep it simple. Besides, they all have tasty fruits regardless of the botanical names bestowed on them.

**Uses:** The fruits can be picked and eaten fresh. In areas where there is an abundance of fruits, they can be harvested to make jams, pie fillings, or used to decorate icing on cakes. Leave plenty behind for the critters.

# DARROW'S BLUEBERRY
*Vaccinium darrowii*

**Also called:** Southern highbush blueberry, scrub blueberry

**Nativity:** Native

**Florida range:** From Collier, Hendry, and St. Lucie Counties north throughout most of peninsular Florida and across the Florida Panhandle

**Habitat:** Low, scrubby flatwoods, sandhills, and scrub

**Description:** Darrow's blueberry forms extensive colonies with plants bearing elliptic leaves that are pale green below and darker above, with margins often inrolled. Small, somewhat cylindric flowers are white, tinged with pink or red. Globose fruits ripen blue and measure about ⅜" wide.

**Cautions:** This species lives in chigger and tick habitat, so wear long pants with shoes and socks and stuff your pant legs into your socks before spraying them with a repellent that contains DEET or picaridin as the primary ingredient. It's still wise to check yourself for ticks after you arrive home, especially for tiny deer ticks that can transmit Lyme disease to humans.

**Comments:** This species was named to honor blueberry pioneer Bill Darrow of Vermont for his work in improving the size and flavor of blueberries for commercial production.

**Uses:** Ripe fruits can be picked and eaten or added to cereal, fruit salads, and ice cream, blended into shakes and smoothies, or any other way you would normally use blueberries.

## SHINY BLUEBERRY
*Vaccinium myrsinites*

**Also called:** Evergreen blueberry
**Nativity:** Native
**Florida range:** Throughout all of mainland Florida except for mainland Monroe County
**Habitat:** Scrubby flatwoods, pinelands, sand-pine scrub, and rosemary balds
**Description:** A small, shrubby species averaging 12"–30" tall with glossy, elliptic leaves to about ⅜" long and ¼" wide with slightly serrulate margins. Small, white to pink or red flowers produce small, oval blueberries to about ¼" wide or less.
**Cautions:** It is not so much an issue in South Florida, but this and other blueberry species live in habitats where ticks are present. See Cautions for the previous species.
**Comments:** Of the 5 species of native blueberries in Florida, this is the most widespread species in the state.
**Uses:** Ripe fruits can be picked and eaten fresh or added to cereal, fruit salads, and ice cream, blended into shakes and smoothies, or any other way you would normally use blueberries.

# EUPHORBIACEAE (SPURGE FAMILY)

## STINGING NETTLE
*Cnidoscolus stimulosus*

**Also called:** Tread-softly, finger-rot, spurge nettle
**Nativity:** Native
**Florida range:** Throughout all of Florida
**Habitat:** Pinelands, beach dunes, scrub, sandhills, and disturbed sites
**Description:** Herbaceous perennial averaging 6"–24" tall with stems and deeply lobed leaves covered with stinging hairs. White, 5-lobed flowers are about ½" across, followed by 3-lobed, hairy fruits.
**Cautions:** The entire plant is covered with hairs that will cause intense and painful burning when contact is made with bare skin. It is important to not scratch the affected area but

wash it with soap and water as soon as possible to remove the chemicals responsible for the burning. Cover the affected area with tape, then pull it off to remove any remaining hairs. The burning dissipates after about 30 minutes, but creams that contain hydrocortisone might provide some relief sooner. Seek immediate medical help if you are having an allergic reaction. Symptoms include tightness in the chest or throat, difficulty breathing, swelling of the mouth, tongue, or lips, vomiting, and appearance of a rash in areas of the skin not contacted by the plant.

**Comments:** This species is one of the larval host plants of the echo moth, but if you want to attract echo moths, they feed on many other user-friendly plants, so there is no need to purposely propagate stinging nettle.

**Uses:** The thick roots of this plant are edible and may extend far away from the main stem, especially on older plants growing in sandy soil. Clean the roots and then cut them into sections before placing in a pot of boiling water. During the boiling process, it is recommended to pour the water off 2 or 3 times to remove any toxins. The finished product will taste similar to potatoes. The leaves of the related, nearly tree-like species called chaya or tree spinach (*Cnidoscolus aconitifolius*) are commonly cooked as greens in many parts of the world. It is not native to Florida but has been found naturalized in Broward County. Stems root very easily, so it was likely the result of discarded stems from a cultivated plant.

# FABACEAE (PEA FAMILY)

## GROUNDNUT
*Apios americana*

**Also called:** American groundnut, Indian potato, hopniss, cinnamon vine
**Nativity:** Native
**Florida range:** Throughout nearly all of mainland Florida
**Habitat:** Moist forests, river bank thickets, freshwater marshes, meadows, and stream banks
**Description:** A low-growing vine with compound leaves bearing 3–7 (usually 3) lanceolate leaflets. Flowers are brownish purple and measure about ½" wide. Seeds are produced in elongate, flattened legumes.
**Cautions:** Medical research indicates that the tubers should not be eaten raw due to toxins (protease inhibitors) that may cause diabetes, kidney stones, and other health issues. These toxins are rendered harmless by cooking.
**Comments:** The underground tubers of groundnut have long been a traditional, staple food among indigenous North American tribes within its range, which extends from southern Canada south to Florida and west to Colorado. It is grown commercially in Japan as a food crop.
**Uses:** The underground tubers can be washed and peeled, then baked, steamed, or boiled. Serve as you would white potatoes.

## PERENNIAL PEANUT
*Arachis glabrata*

**Also called:** Grassnut, rhizoma peanut
**Nativity:** Introduced from South America
**Florida range:** Currently vouchered in 20 counties from the far western Panhandle south through the peninsula to Miami-Dade County, but likely occurs in other counties
**Habitat:** Roadsides, fallow fields, groves, and other disturbed sites
**Description:** Mat-forming, rhizomatous, herbaceous perennial with compound leaves, each bearing 4 linear-lanceolate to oblanceolate leaflets to 1½" long and ½" wide. Showy, yellow to yellow-orange flowers average about ⅝" wide. It does not produce seedpods.
**Cautions:** It is reported that eating the leaves in quantity can have a laxative effect, so dine accordingly.
**Comments:** Perennial peanut is planted as a forage crop and a nitrogen-fixing cover crop in farm fields, where it can spread by rhizomes into adjacent natural areas or roadsides. Fortunately, it seldom sets seed or it would likely become a major weed. It is becoming popular as a groundcover for residential landscapes and parking lot islands, but it is also being carefully monitored by the Florida Invasive Species Council for possible listing if it begins to invade and adversely affect natural habitats.
**Uses:** The flowers of perennial peanut are widely eaten wherever it is cultivated, and they have a flavor that somewhat resembles peanuts or beans. If you are collecting flowers in or near a farm field, it would be wise to wash them with soapy water to rid them of any insecticides or other chemical sprays. Tender young leaves can be cooked as a potherb.

## FLORIDA KEYS BLACKBEAD
*Pithecellobium keyense*

**Also called:** Blackbead, Keys blackbead
**Nativity:** Native
**Florida range:** From Martin County down the eastern coast to Miami-Dade County and the Monroe County mainland and Keys
**Habitat:** Pinelands, hammock margins, and coastal strand
**Description:** Woody shrub or small tree to 18' tall. The alternate, evenly bipinnate leaves have 2 or 4 obliquely obovate leaflets that reach 1"–1½" long and ½"–⅝" wide. Pale pink or white flower heads measure about ¾" in diameter and produce coiled pods to 4" long that split open to reveal black seeds with a red aril.
**Cautions:** Watch out for the sharp thorns on the stems.
**Comments:** This is a state-listed threatened species on the northern edge of its range in Florida. It is more common in the Florida Keys than on the mainland but is locally common within Everglades National Park (Miami-Dade and Monroe Counties). Two other species, *Pithecellobium bahamense* (lower Keys only) and *Pithecellobium unguis-cati*, are also native to Florida.
**Uses:** The red aril surrounding the black seeds is sweet-tasting and can be harvested once the pods split open after ripening.

# TAMARIND
*Tamarindus indica*

**Also called:** Indian tamarind

**Nativity:** Introduced from tropical Africa

**Florida range:** Naturalized and vouchered in Manatee, Lee, Collier, and Broward Counties and the Monroe County Keys but probably occurs in other South Florida counties as well

**Habitat:** Invasive in forests located near cultivated trees

**Description:** Large tree to 30' tall or more with a dense canopy of compound leaves bearing narrowly oblong leaflets, each averaging about ½" long and ¼" wide. Flowers are pinkish white in pendent racemes. The fruits are brown pods with a thin shell that cracks easily when ripe to reveal the brown, sweet-tart pulp surrounding the seeds.

**Cautions:** The pulp in unripe fruits is extremely tart.

**Comments:** Tamarind is widely cultivated in tropical and warm temperate regions worldwide, especially in the Indian subcontinent where it is grown commercially as a food crop. It is sparingly naturalized in Florida and is most commonly found invading forests in the Florida Keys where the seeds are transported from cultivated trees into hammocks by hungry raccoons. It has many uses worldwide and is a key ingredient in chutney. The tender new leaves are cooked and eaten in some countries, the wood is widely used in cabinetry and bowls, plus it has many uses in folk medicine, such as to relieve fever and constipation and help lower cholesterol. Chickens fed tamarind pulp have been shown to lay eggs that are lower in cholesterol. As a food, tamarind fruits are most popular in Africa, India, Mexico, and the Philippines. In Florida it is sometimes seen in cultivation as a shade tree or backyard fruit tree, but if you find naturalized trees in native habitats, carry the seeds out with you so you do not contribute to its spread.

**Uses:** The fruits are ripe when the outer shell cracks easily when pressed between the fingers (in South Florida the fruits ripen late spring into early summer). The brown pulp surrounding the seeds is edible fresh and can be described as sweet and pleasingly tart. The tartness varies due to degree of ripeness and individual trees or cultivars. Tamarind pulp is widely used to make chutney and is used in the Philippines to make a Filipino beef, pork, fish, or vegetable soup, called *sinigang*, which was rated the best-tasting vegetable soup by TasteAtlas. Recipes for chutney and *sinigang* are available on the internet. Another use in the Bahamas involves adding bruised leaves to a cup of water and allowing it to sit overnight. Strain the water and use it as an eye wash or eye drops to treat eye irritation from colds or infections.

# FAGACEAE (OAK FAMILY)

## LIVE OAK
*Quercus virginiana*

**Also called:** Evergreen oak
**Nativity:** Native
**Florida range:** Throughout all of Florida
**Habitat:** Xeric and mesic forests, pinelands, and hammocks
**Description:** Large tree reaching 60' tall or more with large, wide-spreading branches and deeply fissured bark. Dark green leaves are generally obovate to oblanceolate with entire margins or with 1–3 teeth on each side, averaging 1½"–2½" long and about ¾" wide or more. Acorns have a hemispheric cup on top and measure about ½" long and wide.
**Cautions:** The acorn weevil drills holes in acorns and lays eggs inside for the larvae to feed on the kernel.
**Comments:** Live oak is the only oak species that ranges throughout Florida, although it is very rare in the upper Florida Keys. There are 26 native species of oaks in Florida plus 15 naturally occurring hybrids, so it is the most prolific and diverse genus of trees in the state. Most become trees but some species remain shrubby. All produce edible acorns. *Quercus virginiana* was dubbed "live oak" because it retains its leaves all year, while other oak species

drop their leaves in wintertime and appear to be "dead." Acorns can be harvested when mature (brown), but inspect each one and discard those that have a small hole drilled into them by adult acorn weevils (see Cautions).

**Uses:** Although some oaks produce acorns that are edible raw, most are somewhat bitter due to their tannin content. This can be easily remedied by boiling. Place the whole acorns in a stainless-steel pot and cover with water, discarding any that float, and boil for about 10 minutes. During that time, bring a second pot of water to a boil and then transfer the acorns to the second pot of boiling water for an additional 10 minutes. Drain, then spread the acorns out on a cookie sheet and bake at 175°F for about 15–20 minutes. Once cooled you can use a nutcracker or a small hammer to crack the outer shell and remove the kernel. The cooked kernels can be eaten whole, like nuts, or ground into a mealy texture in a blender and then mixed with pancake batter before cooking, or added to biscuit or oatmeal cookie dough before baking. Another option is to make pemmican, which is a forager's survival food. To make one version of pemmican, follow the recipe below.

## RECIPE

**Peanut Butter Pemmican**

2 cups dried beef jerky
1 cup dried fruit (blueberries, apricots, apples—your choice)
1 cup acorn meal
¼ cup peanut butter (either creamy or crunchy)
2 tablespoons honey

*Note:* To make acorn meal, place shelled, ripe acorns in a blender and blend on high until it has a mealy texture.

1. Place the beef jerky in a blender and blend on medium speed first, and then on high to reduce it to a mealy powder.

2. Add the dried fruit of choice and the acorn meal to the beef jerky powder, then blend on high.

3. Place the peanut butter in a microwave and heat until it has melted.

4. Add the honey and peanut butter to the meal in the blender and blend at medium speed until thoroughly mixed.

5. Form into balls (about golf ball size) and refrigerate to harden.

*Note:* Pemmican will keep unrefrigerated for weeks, so it is a perfect survival food for long-distance hiking, paddling, and other outdoor adventures. Or it is perfectly suited as a snack while curled up on the couch watching an old movie on television.

# JUGLANDACEAE (WALNUT FAMILY)

## WATER HICKORY
*Carya aquatica*

**Also called:** Bitter pecan, swamp hickory, water pignut
**Nativity:** Native
**Florida range:** Across the Florida Panhandle and south in the peninsula to Lee, Hendry, and Palm Beach Counties
**Habitat:** River floodplains, bottomland forests, and levees
**Description:** Deciduous tree to 60' tall or more with exfoliating bark. Alternate, compound leaves typically produce 9 or 11 lanceolate leaflets 2½"–4" long and up to 1" wide. The margins are normally serrate, but this is not always obvious. The fruits are bronze, brown, or black with a 4-ridged outer shell that splits open to the base when mature.
**Cautions:** The nuts can be very difficult to crack.
**Comments:** Foragers who decide to look for water hickory nuts should wear clothing they don't mind getting wet.
**Uses:** The chocolate-brown kernels can be eaten when mature.

## PIGNUT HICKORY
*Carya glabra*

**Also called:** Smoothbark hickory, sweet pignut
**Nativity:** Native
**Florida range:** Throughout the Florida Panhandle and northern peninsula south to Charlotte, Highlands, Osceola, and Brevard Counties
**Habitat:** River floodplains and on dry, sandy soils
**Description:** Deciduous tree to 50' tall or more with smooth or exfoliating bark, sometimes in diamond patterns. Alternate, compound leaves bear 3–7 lanceolate, elliptic, or ovate leaflets measuring 3"–6" long and 1"–2" wide, with serrate margins. The tan to reddish-brown fruits are somewhat pear-shaped and produce tan, obovoid to ellipsoid nuts.
**Comments:** This species is found in mesic forests, edges of hardwood swamps, and in well-drained, sandy soils.
**Uses:** The nuts are edible but can be bitter.

## PECAN
*Carya illinoinensis*

**Also called:** Illinois hickory
**Nativity:** Introduced (native from Alabama to Texas and across much of the eastern United States)
**Florida range:** Naturalized throughout the Florida Panhandle and vouchered in Levy and Orange Counties in peninsular Florida
**Habitat:** River floodplains, stream banks, and on well-drained soils
**Description:** Large, deciduous tree to 100' tall or more bearing pinnately compound leaves to 20" long with 11–17 lanceolate leaflets. Flowers are inconspicuous, with male and female flowers produced on the same tree. Fruits are oblong nuts enclosed in a thin shell that splits open when mature.
**Comments:** Pecan is a larval host plant of the gray hairstreak butterfly. The sweet, edible nuts provide food for many mammals and is the most widely cultivated of all the hickories.
**Uses:** Mature nuts can be cracked to reveal the kernels, which can be eaten fresh or added to salads and other dishes where you would normally use pecans.

# MOCKERNUT HICKORY
*Carya tomentosa*

**Also called:** White hickory, hognut, bullnut
**Nativity:** Native
**Florida range:** Scattered across the Florida Panhandle and south in the peninsula to Citrus, Lake, and Volusia Counties
**Habitat:** Bottomland forests, stream banks, and open glades
**Description:** Deciduous tree to 60' tall or more with pinnately compound, pubescent leaves that turn bright yellow in the fall. The odd-pinnate leaves have 7–9 lanceolate-elliptic to obovate-elliptic leaflets up to 6" long and 2" wide. Male and female flowers are produced on the same tree, with the male flowers in pendent catkins. Ovoid to obovoid fruits are 2"–3" long and slightly narrower in width, separating when ripe to release slightly compressed, somewhat 4-angled nuts with edible kernels.
**Cautions:** The kernels are described as "barely edible" by some foragers.
**Comments:** The wood is highly prized for firewood, charcoal, and smoking meats, especially ham.
**Uses:** The semi-sweet kernels can be eaten fresh.

# BLACK WALNUT
*Juglans nigra*

**Also called:** Eastern black walnut, American black walnut
**Nativity:** Native
**Florida range:** Scattered across the Panhandle and northern Florida from Escambia County to Bradford and Nassau Counties
**Habitat:** Rich, moist woods
**Description:** Large, deciduous tree to 75' tall or more with widely spreading branches. Alternate, compound leaves can reach 24" long with 15–23 ovate-oblong to ovate-lanceolate leaflets up to 5" long and 2" wide. The spherical fruits are about 2" wide.
**Cautions:** The shell of the nut is extremely hard and may take a hammer or vice to crack. The husk is high in tannins and toxins. The fruits may contain huskfly maggots.
**Comments:** This species is the preferred larval host plant of the beautiful luna moth and regal moth. The kernels make up a significant portion of the diet of the fox squirrel and are high in protein.
**Uses:** If you can manage to crack the hard nuts open, the kernel is edible.

# KRAMERIACEAE (RATANY FAMILY)

## TRAILING RATANY
*Krameria lanceolata*

**Also called:** Sandspur, mountain bur
**Nativity:** Native
**Florida range:** Okaloosa, Walton, and Liberty Counties in the Florida Panhandle, and from Suwannee, Columbia, and Clay Counties south to Hillsborough, Polk, and Highlands Counties in the northern and central peninsula
**Habitat:** Pine flatwoods and open, grassy habitats
**Description:** This hemiparasitic species has hairy, spreading stems with sessile, lanceolate, hairy leaves. Each leaf averages ½"–1" long and ⅛"–¼" wide. The wine-red flowers are about ½" wide; spherical fruits are covered with sharp spines.

**Cautions:** Herbal teas or other decoctions of this plant should not be taken by women in early stages of pregnancy because of its use in the Caribbean as an abortifacient.

**Comments:** The name sandspur is sometimes used in Florida for this species due to the sharp spines on the fruits, but that name is most often associated with grasses in the genus *Cenchrus*, which are well-known to anyone who has ever walked barefoot in Florida.

**Uses:** In tropical America and the Caribbean, the astringent stems are chewed to whiten and strengthen the teeth, and a leaf or root decoction is taken to ease menstruation, promote easier childbirth, ease intestinal irritations, and relieve liver and kidney problems. Always keep in mind that these uses are regarded as bush medicine and are not proven to be effective by modern medical research.

# LAMIACEAE (MINT FAMILY)

## AMERICAN BEAUTYBERRY
*Callicarpa americana*

**Also called:** French mulberry
**Nativity:** Native
**Florida range:** Throughout all of Florida
**Habitat:** Pinelands, forest margins, and coastal plains
**Description:** Woody shrub 4'–6' tall with opposite, ovate to elliptic, toothed, aromatic leaves covered with coarse hairs. The leaves average 2"–4" long and 1¼"–2¼" wide. Pink (rarely white) clusters of axillary flowers produce showy clusters of pinkish-purple (rarely white) fruits.
**Cautions:** Concentrated root decoctions can cause an immediate evacuation of the bowels.
**Comments:** The leaves contain high levels of insect-repelling terpenoids and can be crushed and rubbed on the skin as a natural mosquito repellent. However, it is only effective at repelling mosquitoes while sitting outside on your patio, not when standing among mangroves in the Everglades amid dense swarms of salt marsh mosquitoes in the summer, when running and screaming are optional. The leaves have also been shown to produce

anticancer activity in humans. The fruits are a favorite food of birds, especially quail and American robins.

**Uses:** American beautyberry has a long history of medicinal uses, but its principle use as a food is in beautyberry jelly. Eaten fresh, the ripe fruits are somewhat astringent and are survival food at best. Native Americans used a medicinal root, fruit, and leaf tea to treat dysentery, upset stomach, and colic and in sweat baths for fevers, arthritis, rheumatism, colds, and even malaria.

## RECIPE

**Beautyberry Jelly**

1 quart ripe beautyberry fruits
3 cups granulated sugar (try turbinado sugar)
2 tablespoons fresh lemon or lime juice
1 (1.75-ounce) packet of fruit pectin
5 sterilized 8-ounce canning jars

1. Wash the raw berries in a colander and place them in a large, stainless-steel pot. Add water to cover (about 6 cups). Bring the water to a boil, lower the heat, and simmer uncovered for 20–30 minutes.

2. Pour the juice through a strainer into another cooking pot (you should have about 5 cups of juice). Add sugar, stirring until dissolved. Add lemon or lime juice and the packet of pectin. Bring to a low boil, stirring continuously until thickened.

3. Pour into sterilized jars and let sit until cool, then screw on lids and place in refrigerator. Enjoy, but give some to friends and neighbors, too.

## SPOTTED BEEBALM
*Monarda punctata*

**Also called:** Horsemint, dotted horsemint
**Nativity:** Native
**Florida range:** Throughout mainland Florida south to Collier and Palm Beach Counties
**Habitat:** Pinelands, sandhills, scrub, and disturbed sites, including roadsides
**Description:** Spotted beebalm typically reaches 12"–30" tall, with toothed, aromatic, 2"–3" leaves. Hairy, purple-dotted, yellow (or white) flowers are in whorls subtended by pale to showy, pinkish-violet bracts.
**Cautions:** This species can be weedy in cultivation. Although it attracts bees, they attack people only when defending their hives and pose no threat when visiting flowers for nectar or pollen.
**Comments:** Spotted beebalm is excellent at attracting bees, butterflies, and other pollinators. It is locally common throughout most of Florida and can be seen growing along roadsides.
**Uses:** Fresh leaves soaked in cold water are consumed to relieve back pain, inflammation, fever, and chills. Native Americans used a decoction from the leaves to ward off rheumatism, relieve headache, coughs, fevers, and chest congestion, plus to induce perspiration. Crushed leaves and flowers were used as a perfume. Raw or cooked leaves have a strong, aromatic flavor and can be used to flavor salads and other dishes. The leaves can be boiled fresh or dried to make a flavorful hot tea (add honey instead of processed sugar as a sweetener).

## WILD PENNYROYAL
*Piloblephis rigida (*formerly *Satureja rígida)*

**Also called:** Wild mint, Florida pennyroyal

**Nativity:** Native

**Florida range:** Throughout most all of peninsular Florida (absent from the Panhandle and Florida Keys)

**Habitat:** Sandy pockets in pine rocklands, pine flatwoods, sandhills, and scrub

**Description:** Woody perennial subshrub typically reaching 8"–12" tall but may be taller, with spreading or ascending, leafy stems lined with needle-like, fragrant leaves to ½" long. Small, lavender flowers are dotted with purple on the lip and are produced on the tips of the stems.

**Cautions:** Wiping your eyes with your hands after crushing the leaves will cause a burning sensation.

**Comments:** This species was once thought to be endemic to Florida until it was discovered in southeastern Georgia and the Bahamas. The plant is known to have been used by the Miccosukee tribe in the Big Cypress National Preserve to treat "cow creek sickness" (diarrhea caused by drinking polluted water).

**Uses:** The fresh stems with leaves (not dried) make a delightful, minty tea. Simply boil the stems and leaves in a cupful of water for 5 minutes, then allow it to steep for another 10 minutes or more, sweeten with honey, and enjoy hot or on ice. If the tea is too strong, dilute it with water. Small sprigs can be added to other teas, such as chamomile or green tea, as an extra flavoring.

Florida betony rhizomes

# FLORIDA BETONY
*Stachys floridana*

**Also called:** Rattlesnake weed, Florida hedgenettle, wild radish
**Nativity:** Native
**Florida range:** Throughout mainland Florida
**Habitat:** Pinelands, sandhills, and disturbed sites, especially roadsides
**Description:** Florida betony typically reaches 10"–12" tall with square, hairy stems. Flowers are produced in whorls up the stems. Leaves are opposite, to 2" long and ½" wide, with toothed margins. The underground rhizomes have been described as resembling a pearl necklace, a rattlesnake's rattle, or some sort of grub worm. Try not to envision grub worms when eating them!
**Cautions:** Very weedy in cultivation, spreading quickly from seed and underground rhizomes. Although it is regarded as a cherished wildflower by native-plant lovers in Florida, it is classified as a noxious weed outside its natural range, so it is strongly advised to grow this species in a pot where it can be kept under some semblance of control.
**Comments:** Florida betony is often found colonizing roadsides and is usually abundant where you find it. Use a spade or grub hoe to harvest the underground rhizomes in spring or early summer, because by late summer and fall, the rhizomes may have become soft and inedible.
**Uses:** Eaten raw, the crunchy nutlets on the rhizomes have a flavor reminiscent of radishes or water chestnuts. The flavor has also been described as "bland and slightly sweet." Include the nutlets in salads, soups, or stews, or eat them out of hand as a snack while hiking, but wash them first. Other species are popular in parts of Asia and Europe and are eaten both as a food source and for medicinal purposes, but none of the medicinal claims are supported by medical research.

# LAURACEAE (LAUREL FAMILY)

## LOVE VINE
*Cassytha filiformis*

**Also called:** Devil's gut, angel hair, noodles
**Nativity:** Native
**Florida range:** From Hillsborough, Polk, Osceola, and Brevard Counties south through the Florida Keys; disjunct in Franklin County
**Habitat:** Often seen as a parasite on roadside trees and shrubs, but also found parasitizing trees and shrubs in pinelands, sandhills, forest margins, and other open, sunny habitats
**Description:** Parasitic vine with orange to greenish, leafless stems that may entirely engulf the host plant. The stems reach about ⅛" thick with globose flowers to ⅛" wide and globose white fruits to about ¼" wide.
**Cautions:** According to Dr. Dan Austin (1943–2015), the vine contains an alkaloid called laurotetanine, which can be fatal if consumed in large quantities.
**Comments:** Love vine can be mistaken for members of the unrelated morning-glory genus *Cuscuta* (dodders), but the stems of love vine are thicker and the flowers and fruits are vastly different. Love vine has a history of medicinal uses as an herbal tea, including cooking the vine with leaves of gumbo limbo (*Bursera simaruba*) to brew a potion that makes couples fall in love. Dr. Julia Morton (1912–1996) reported that the vine is also cooked with

cure-for-all (*Pluchea carolinensis*) and used as a bath 9 days after women give birth. A tea is brewed from the stems in the Bahamas and consumed by men as an aphrodisiac, without any proof that it works. In parts of its native range, it is also believed that it promotes hair growth or prevents hair loss. Other folk medicine and bush medicine uses of the tea are to cure headaches and stomachaches, relieve the symptoms of colds, and treat high blood pressure.

**Uses:** The fragrant stems are edible in small amounts, and an herbal tea can be brewed. Take a handful of stems and boil them in water for 10 minutes, then steep for 20 minutes. Cream and sugar are sometimes added, just as you would in coffee.

# LANCEWOOD
*Damburneya coriacea (*formerly *Nectandra coriacea* and *Ocotea coriacea)*

**Also called:** Sweet torchwood (Bahamas)
**Nativity:** Native
**Florida range:** Volusia and Collier Counties south along both coasts into the Florida Keys; disjunct in Highlands County
**Habitat:** Hammocks
**Description:** Evergreen tropical tree to 25' tall or more with smooth, light gray bark and leathery, lanceolate leaves 4"–5" long and 1½"–2" wide, fragrant when crushed. Fragrant, 6-lobed flowers are about ⅜" wide, followed by oval or subglobose fruits to about ⅜" wide, ripening dark blue to black, atop a red or yellow calyx base.
**Comments:** Lancewood is one of the more common trees in the hammocks of South Florida, especially in southern Miami-Dade County.
**Uses:** The fruits can be picked and eaten but are not very flavorful. The leaves can be dried, crushed, and added to a pot of boiling water, then steeped for 20 minutes to brew an aromatic tea.

## AVOCADO
*Persea americana*

**Also called:** Alligator pear

**Nativity:** Introduced from the tropical Americas

**Florida range:** Though vouchered as being naturalized in Hernando, Lee, and Miami-Dade Counties, this species is far more widespread in Florida than vouchered specimens indicate.

**Habitat:** Within regions in Florida where it is cultivated, it can be found as an invader in hammocks, usually within walking distance for a raccoon from a residential tree or a commercial grove.

**Description:** Large to medium tree with spreading branches and elliptic, dark green leaves averaging 6"–8" long and 3"–4" wide. Fruits vary widely in shape and size, from oblong to pear-shaped, smooth or coarse skin, and ripening green, purple, or black. The flesh on the inside is yellow.

**Cautions:** A recent report published in 2018 by the Food and Drug Administration found that 1 in 5 imported avocados tested positive on the outer skin for *Listeria monocytogrenes*, which can cause a variety of health issues, including nausea, vomiting, and diarrhea. When buying avocados in marketplaces, wash them with dishwashing detergent when you arrive home, and wash your hands after handling them just to be safe.

**Comments:** There is a booming avocado industry in South Florida, with thousands of acres of groves. However, a disease called laurel wilt has caused the death of many trees in recent years, both in commercial groves and residential landscapes. Raccoons and other animals are responsible for carrying fruits from cultivated trees into forest preserves, where the seeds germinate and grow alongside native trees.

**Uses:** Ripe fruits can be peeled and eaten, typically with salt and pepper, but foragers lucky enough to find a fruiting tree will be happy just to eat the fruit as is. Fruits fall and ripen on the ground, but mature fruits can be picked and allowed to ripen at home, or in your backpack if you are hiking. Avocados are used in guacamole, salsas, salads, mashed on toast for breakfast, added to tacos, or even used to make avocado wine. Although avocado wine sounds god-awful, it is actually a very pleasant dry wine. Visit Schnebly Winery in Homestead, Florida, to give it a taste.

## RED BAY
*Persea borbonia* var. *borbonia*

**Also called:** Laurel tree
**Nativity:** Native
**Florida range:** Throughout all of Florida
**Habitat:** Xeric and mesic forests, wooded swamps, hardwood hammocks, and pinelands
**Description:** Evergreen tree to 50' tall or more with ascending branches and alternate, lanceolate leaves averaging 3"–4" long and ¾"–1" wide. The leaves are slightly rusty or pale pubescent below and aromatic when crushed. Small, yellowish flowers produce ⅜", bluish-black fruits (drupes).
**Cautions:** It is reported that the Seminole used a concentrated infusion of red bay leaves as an abortifacient, so women in early stages of pregnancy should avoid its consumption.
**Comments:** A disease called laurel wilt has been killing red bay trees in Florida and across the southeastern states, and has switched over to its relative, the avocado (*Persea americana*), causing losses of many avocado trees in South Florida groves. Swamp bay (*Persea palustris*) is similar to red bay and also occurs in Florida. Silk bay (*Persea borbonia* var. *humilis*) occurs in central Florida south to Collier County. Some leaves of red bay may be deformed by the larvae of the red bay psillid, and the leaf deformity is so common it has become a means of identifying red bay trees.
**Uses:** The leaves can be dried and used to brew an herbal tea (see Cautions), or fresh leaves can be used to flavor spaghetti sauce and any other dishes where commercial bay leaf (*Laurus nobilis*) is used.

# MALPIGHIACEAE (MALPIGHIA FAMILY)

## LOCUSTBERRY
*Byrsonima lucida*

**Also called:** Sweet Margaret (Bahamas), plum berry (Bahamas), goose berry (Virgin Islands)
**Nativity:** Native
**Florida range:** Miami-Dade County and the Monroe County Keys
**Habitat:** Tropical hardwood hammocks, pine rocklands, and rocky flats
**Description:** Locustberry can become a tree to 18' in hammocks or occurs as a shrub in pine rockland habitat. The obovate leaves average ½"–1" long and up to about ½" wide. The flowers reach ⅜" wide and open white, turning pink and then red as they age, forming multicolored clusters. The round, brownish-orange fruits are about ⅜" wide.
**Cautions:** Green, unripe fruits are astringent and have a laxative effect if eaten.
**Comments:** This is a relatively common understory tree in the pine rocklands of southern Miami-Dade County, where it is kept shrubby by fire. In hammocks, especially in the Florida Keys, it can become a tree. It is commonly cultivated by native-plant enthusiasts in southern Florida and is sold by local nurseries that specialize in native plants. The fruits are savored by birds.
**Uses:** Ripe fruits are brownish orange in color and can be picked fresh and eaten. The flavor has been described as tasting like cranberries, while others compare them to soap. I would describe them as being pleasantly tart. In the West Indies the bark is brewed into a tea and used medicinally to treat sore throats. According to the book *Bush Medicine of the Bahamas* (McCormack et al., 2011), a decoction is made in the Bahamas from locustberry, five finger (*Tabebuia bahamensis*), gumbo limbo (*Bursera simaruba*), strongback (*Bourreria succulenta*), love vine (*Cassytha filiformis*), and wild pine (*Tillandsia* spp.), which are boiled together and strained, then sugar, brandy, and evaporated milk are added before the decoction is allowed to sit for several weeks. It is then consumed by men as an aphrodisiac to "build up energy in the body." No word on its effectiveness.

# MALVACEAE (MALLOW FAMILY)

## SLIPPERY BURR
*Corchorus siliquosus*

**Also called:** Broomweed
**Nativity:** Native
**Florida range:** Broward, Miami-Dade, Collier, and Monroe (mainland and Keys) Counties
**Habitat:** Pinelands, glade edges, hammock margins, beaches, and roadsides
**Description:** Annual or short-lived perennial averaging 12"–36" tall but may be taller. Elliptic-ovate leaves have serrate margins, measuring ½"–1" long and half as wide. Yellow flowers are about ⅝" wide.
**Comments:** This species is infrequently encountered within its range in South Florida and is not in the Florida nursery trade, perhaps due to it being an annual or short-lived perennial.
**Uses:** The tender young leaves can be cooked as greens, and the dried leaves are brewed as an herbal tea in tropical American countries. The name broomweed relates to the plant being used to sweep the floor.

## SLEEPY MORNING
*Waltheria indica*

**Also called:** Velvet leaf, monkey bush
**Nativity:** Native
**Florida range:** Pinellas, Hillsborough, Lake, and St. Lucie Counties south into the Florida Keys
**Habitat:** Pinelands, sandhills, scrub, beaches, forest margins, and disturbed sites
**Description:** Subshrub 3'–6' tall with alternate, toothed, tomentose, ovate to oblong leaves that average 1"–2" long and ½"–1" wide. Flowers are about ⅛" wide, crowded in mostly sessile, axillary inflorescences.
**Cautions:** In parts of its range in Africa, an infusion of *Waltheria* is used as an abortifacient, so herbal tea made from any species should be avoided by women in early stages of pregnancy.
**Comments:** The name sleepy morning relates to the flowers opening late in the morning, and has nothing to do with sedative properties. *Waltheria indica* has a long list of medicinal uses across its range in both developed and developing countries. It is traditionally used to treat persistent coughs, diarrhea, rheumatism, impotence, female sterility, bladder ailments, malaria, typhoid fever, and other maladies. It is also claimed to be an aphrodisiac, without medical backing. Another species, *Waltheria bahamensis*, also occurs in Florida and is characterized by a spreading, prostrate growth habit. Leaves and flowers look similar.
**Uses:** A somewhat astringent herbal tea can be brewed from a combination of the flowers, dried leaves, and young stems. Drink it hot or on ice, sweetened with honey.

# MARANTACEAE (ARROWROOT FAMILY)

## ALLIGATOR FLAG
*Thalia geniculata*

**Also called:** Fire flag
**Nativity:** Native
**Florida range:** Throughout much of peninsular Florida into the central Panhandle
**Habitat:** Freshwater wetlands, including sloughs, wooded swamps, canals, river and stream shorelines, ditches, ponds, and lakes
**Description:** Herbaceous perennial averaging 5'–9' tall that is easily identified by its broad, lanceolate leaf blade held at an angle and reaching 3' long and 1' wide. The odd-shaped flowers have 3 purple petals, 3 small sepals, and hang in pairs on zigzagging stems.
**Cautions:** American alligators and cottonmouth moccasins live in this plant's habitat, so use due caution.
**Comments:** The name alligator flag comes from alligators pushing through thickets of the plants, causing the leaves to wave like flags. Alligator flag forms extensive colonies in freshwater wetlands, including wooded swamps, and is almost always found growing in standing water. Also look for it in canals, roadside ditches, and along margins of ponds and lakes.
**Uses:** The tender, very young leaves and shoots can be boiled as a green. The roots can also be boiled and eaten, turning pink when cooked, and have a flavor that has been described as "earthy." I would consider them survival food at best. Another popular use of the plant throughout its range in the tropical Americas is to wrap fish and meats in the leaves to cook over coals, in the same manner banana leaves are used. Heating the leaves with hot water prior to wrapping makes them more pliable.

# MORACEAE (MULBERRY FAMILY)

## STRANGLER FIG
*Ficus aurea*

**Also called:** Golden fig (Bahamas)

**Nativity:** Native

**Florida range:** Volusia, Polk, and Hillsborough Counties south through the Florida Keys

**Habitat:** Coastal and inland hammocks, often seen as an epiphyte growing in the leaf bases of palms and on rough-barked trees

**Description:** Large tree to 80' tall or more with smooth bark and often producing stout aerial roots from the branches that help support their weight. The leaves have short petioles, and the leaf blade averages 4"–5" long and 2"–3" wide but sometimes larger. The figs are sessile, measuring ⅜" wide, ripening dark red.

**Cautions:** If you have a queasy stomach, or are a strict vegan, the fruits may contain larvae of a species of fig wasp, which are so tiny they are rarely seen.

**Comments:** This tree frequently begins life as an epiphyte, growing on other trees or in the boots of cabbage palms where it typically kills its host tree by using a combination of constricting roots, creating dense shade, and competing for nutrients in the soil, but this can take years or even decades. The fig is actually the stem of an inflorescence that surrounds very tiny flowers inside. *Ficus* species are pollinated by specific fig wasps, and the species that pollinates the strangler fig is *Pegoscapus mexicanus*. Fig wasps are small enough to crawl inside the fig, where they pollinate the flowers and lay eggs. The larvae then feed on the fig pulp before pupating into flying adults ready to continue the cycle.

**Uses:** The small figs can be picked and eaten when ripe (purple).

## SHORTLEAF FIG
*Ficus citrifolia*

**Also called:** Wild banyan

**Nativity:** Native

**Florida range:** Collier, Hendry, and Broward Counties south through the Florida Keys (also a disjunct record from Hillsborough County).

**Habitat:** Coastal and inland hammocks; less frequently seen growing as an epiphyte on other trees like the previous species

**Description:** Large, usually deciduous tree (sometimes growing on other trees and palms) to 50' tall or more with stout aerial roots. The leaves average 2½"–5" long and 1½"–3" wide with long petioles and often with a slightly cordate base. The small figs are on ⅜" stalks, differentiating it from the strangler fig.

**Cautions:** See Cautions for the previous species.

**Comments:** The fig wasp that pollinates the shortleaf fig is *Pegoscapus tonduzi*, in case you're interested in knowing which species of fig wasp larvae you may be eating.

**Uses:** The small figs can be picked and eaten when ripe (purple).

## RED MULBERRY
*Morus rubra*

**Also called:** Virginia mulberry
**Nativity:** Native
**Florida range:** Throughout all of mainland Florida (absent from the Florida Keys)
**Habitat:** Hardwood forests, stream and river banks, ditches, and depressions
**Description:** Deciduous, dioecious tree to 40' or more but typically less than 20' tall in Florida. The leaf blades are broadly ovate, sometimes irregularly and deeply lobed, with toothed margins, measuring 5"–7" long and 3"–4" wide. Female trees produce red berries to about ½" long, ripening black or dark purple.
**Cautions:** Eating unripe berries can cause gastrointestinal distress, and the sap from the bark can cause a skin rash in sensitive people.
**Comments:** This is a well-known tree throughout its natural range and elsewhere but is surprisingly only sparingly cultivated in Florida. A more popular mulberry in the Florida nursery trade is the non-native black mulberry (*Morus nigra*), which is far more available than our native red mulberry.
**Uses:** Ripe berries can be harvested and eaten fresh or they can be added to fruit salads, tossed in with your morning breakfast cereal, used as a topping on ice cream, or mixed with sugar and cornmeal to make dumplings. If you have an ample supply of fruits, they can be made into a pie.

**Red Mulberry Pie**

3 cups ripe mulberries, stems removed
1¼ cups granulated sugar
¼ cup all-purpose flour
2 tablespoons butter
1 tablespoon milk
1 pre-made 9-inch double pie crust (or make your own)

1. Preheat oven to 400ºF.

2. In a large bowl, mix berries with the sugar and flour.

3. Pour mixture into the bottom pie crust and dot with butter. Cover with the top pie crust and crimp the edges, then cut several slits in the center.

4. Brush the top pie crust with milk and place in the refrigerator for 30 minutes.

5. Bake the pie in the preheated oven for 15 minutes, then lower the temperature to 350ºF and continue baking for another 30 minutes.

6. Remove from oven and let stand until cool. Slice and serve.

# MUNTINGIACEAE (MUNTINGIA FAMILY)

## STRAWBERRY TREE
*Muntingia calabura*

**Also called:** Cotton candy berry, capulin, Jamaica cherry, Panama berry

**Nativity:** Introduced; native to tropical America

**Florida range:** Naturalized in Collier, Hendry, and Palm Beach Counties south into the Florida Keys

**Habitat:** Woodland margins and disturbed sites

**Description:** Large shrub or small tree, typically reaching about 16' tall but may reach twice that height. The widely spreading branches are held horizontal with toothed, oblong to lanceolate, hairy leaves averaging about 3" long and 1"–2" wide. The ½" flowers have 5 obovate petals and are followed by oval, ⅜", dark pink to red berries.

**Cautions:** People diagnosed with low blood sugar levels should avoid eating the fruits in quantity.

**Comments:** Strawberry tree is cultivated for its edible fruits in tropical and warm temperate regions, including South Florida. It is sparingly naturalized in South Florida where it may be found colonizing disturbed sites or growing along hammock margins. Seeds are spread by birds, iguanas, and small mammals that feast on the fruits. It is fast growing and is sometimes cultivated in developing nations as a source of timber and fuel. It is also widely planted by beekeepers as a source of nectar for commercial beehives. Strawberry tree is sold in South Florida nurseries.

**Uses:** Fruits can be picked and eaten fresh, and have been described as tasting like cotton candy. In some countries the fruits are used to make jams, jellies, and pies. The leaves can also be harvested and brewed as a medicinal tea to relieve headaches, treat prostate problems, reduce swelling, and relieve respiratory problems, but without medical evidence that it is effective. The fruits have been found, however, to reduce blood sugar levels in patients with diabetes.

# MYRICACEAE (BAYBERRY FAMILY)

## WAX MYRTLE
*Morella cerifera (*formerly *Myrica cerifera)*

**Also called:** Southern bayberry
**Nativity:** Native
**Florida range:** Throughout all of Florida
**Habitat:** Pinelands, forested swamps, coastal strand, sandhills, forest margins, and disturbed sites
**Description:** Shrub or small tree to 14' tall or more with coarsely toothed, linear-oblanceolate leaves that are aromatic when crushed. Male and female flowers are on separate plants, produced along the stems. Round, bluish-gray, waxy fruits are about ⅛" wide, clustered along the stems.
**Comments:** One phenomenon worth watching is when hundreds of tree swallows drop from the sky like a tornado of birds and descend on a fruiting wax myrtle in a frenzy of wings and chirping, and then exit in the same manner, leaving the wax myrtle stripped of its fruits.
**Uses:** A widespread use of wax myrtle is to collect large quantities of fruits and boil them in a kettle of water until the wax coating melts and floats to the surface. The wax is then skimmed off, cooled to harden, and used to make fragrant, long-burning, smokeless candles. The leaves can be dried and boiled to make a flavorful tea, or the dried leaves can be crumbled and used to flavor foods.

# MYRSINACEAE (MYRSINE FAMILY)

## MARLBERRY
*Ardisia escallonioides*

**Also called:** Marbleberry, marvelberry
**Nativity:** Native
**Florida range:** Vouchered from Citrus and Flagler Counties south through mainland Florida into the Florida Keys
**Habitat:** Hammocks and pinelands
**Description:** Shrub or small tree typically 8'–14' tall with alternate, dark green, oblanceolate to elliptic leaves averaging 2"–4" long and 1"–2" wide. Fragrant flowers are in terminal clusters, each measuring about ¼" across. Fruits ripen dark purple and measure about ¼" wide.
**Cautions:** The related *Ardisia crenata* and *A. elliptica* are both naturalized in Florida and are listed by the Florida Invasive Species Council as Category I invasive species. Every effort should be taken to eradicate those two species from Florida's natural areas and ban them from cultivation.
**Comments:** The name marlberry is believed to be a transliteration of marbleberry or marvelberry. The leaves have been dried and used by Native Americans either as a tobacco substitute or to flavor tobacco.
**Uses:** The ripe (dark purple) fruits of marlberry can be picked and eaten, and have a pleasantly tart flavor, although some people describe them as "unappealing." Be sure to leave some for the birds.

# MYRTACEAE (MYRTLE FAMILY)

## REDBERRY STOPPER
*Eugenia confusa*

**Also called:** Redberry eugenia

**Nativity:** Native

**Florida range:** Vouchered in Brevard, Martin, and Miami-Dade Counties and the Monroe County Keys

**Habitat:** Coastal hammocks

**Description:** Small to medium-sized tropical tree that averages 18'–30' tall with opposite, stiff, glossy, elliptic-lanceolate leaves with an elongated apex. The leaves average 1½"–2¼" long and ¾"–1" wide, with revolute margins. Flowers are on ½" peduncles, clustered or solitary along the stems, and produce subglobose, scarlet fruits to about ¼" wide.

**Cautions:** Little is known about the potential toxicity of essential oil extracts from members of this genus.

**Comments:** This state-listed endangered species is most common in Florida in hammocks within Coconut Grove in Miami-Dade County. The national champion is growing in a parking lot island at Villa Vizcaya in Coconut Grove. It is sold by nurseries in Miami-Dade County that specialize in Florida native plants, and possibly in other nurseries within its range. White stopper (*Eugenia axillaris*) is common, but the fruits are nearly inedible. Red stopper (*Eugenia rhombea*) is an endangered species from the Florida Keys, and long-stalked stopper (*Mosiera longipes*) is a threatened species native to Miami-Dade County and the Monroe County Keys.

**Uses:** The ripe fruits can be picked and eaten, plus the leaves can be dried, crushed, and boiled to make a pleasant-tasting herbal tea.

## SPANISH STOPPER
*Eugenia foetida*

**Also called:** Boxleaf stopper
**Nativity:** Native
**Florida range:** Brevard and Manatee Counties south along both coasts into the Florida Keys
**Habitat:** Hammocks
**Description:** Small to medium-sized tree to 18' tall or more with opposite, blunt-tipped leaves reaching about 1½" long and 1" wide. Small, white flowers appear in dense clusters at the nodes along the branches and are followed by ¼" fruits that ripen black in the fall.
**Cautions:** Little is known about the potential toxicity of essential oil extracts from members of this genus.
**Comments:** Spanish stopper is most common in the southernmost counties in Florida, where it is frequently grown by native-plant enthusiasts. It is often multi-trunked and used as a tall privacy hedge.
**Uses:** Ripe fruits are edible when fresh.

## SURINAM CHERRY
*Eugenia uniflora*

**Also called:** Pitanga, Brazilian cherry, Suriname cherry
**Nativity:** Introduced from South America
**Florida range:** Naturalized in the lower half of mainland Florida into the Florida Keys
**Habitat:** Mostly invasive in hammocks and disturbed sites
**Description:** Large shrub or small tree to about 20' tall with opposite, glossy, ovate leaves averaging about 1¼" long and ¾" wide with an elongated tip. The leaves are fragrant when crushed (see Cautions). White flowers bear 4 petals with a cluster of stamens in the center, with each flower measuring about ½" wide. Fruits are lobed like tiny pumpkins, ripening red or black, and reaching about ¾" wide.
**Cautions:** Crushed leaves emit a resinous fragrance that has reportedly caused mild respiratory issues in sensitive people. Little is known about the potential toxicity of essential oil extracts from members of this genus.
**Comments:** This species is listed by the Florida Invasive Species Council as a Category I invasive species because it prolifically reseeds in the natural habitats that it invades and is readily spread to new areas by birds and mammals. It is very commonly seen in central and southern Florida as a pruned hedge around homes and shopping mall parking lot islands,

and is grown in home gardens as a tropical fruit tree. The fruits are low in sugar (4 percent) and high in Vitamin C.

**Uses:** The ripe fruits can be eaten fresh and taste far better than any of the native *Eugenia* species. If you forage on Surinam cherry fruits in natural habitats, take the seeds with you so you do not to contribute to its spread. A leaf tea has been used as an alternative medicine to treat diabetes, rheumatism, and arthritis, as well as to modify mood swings and depression. Other uses of the fruit include making jams, jellies, and spreads as well as wine and rum punch.

## RECIPE

**Surinam Cherry Jam**

2 cups Surinam cherries, seeded and mashed
½ cup granulated sugar
2 tablespoons lemon juice

Place the mashed Surinam cherry pulp, sugar, and lemon juice in a stainless-steel pan over medium heat until it reaches a high simmer, then reduce the heat to low and continue simmering while stirring intermittently for about 30 minutes until it thickens. Cool and use as you would any jam.

## SPICEWOOD
*Myrcia neopallens (*formerly *Calyptranthes pallens)*

**Also called:** Pale lidflower
**Nativity:** Native
**Florida range:** Miami-Dade County and the Monroe County Keys
**Habitat:** Tropical hardwood hammocks and occasionally pine rocklands as an understory shrub
**Description:** Shrub or small tree to 18' tall or more with opposite, elliptical to somewhat lanceolate leaves reaching 2½" long and 1¼" wide. The midrib is not raised above the surface of the leaf blade, and the new growth is pinkish in color. Fragrant, ⅜" flowers are in axillary clusters and can cover the entire canopy. Small, oval fruits ripen dark red.
**Comments:** Spicewood is typically a small tree of South Florida's tropical hardwood hammocks and sometimes grows in the company of its close relative, myrtle-of-the-river (*Myrcia zuzygium*), a state-listed endangered species. Both species can be seen growing side by side along the Mahogany Hammock boardwalk in Everglades National Park (foraging is illegal).
**Uses:** The ripe fruits can be picked and eaten fresh, and the leaves can be dried, crushed, and brewed into an herbal tea, which is used medicinally in the West Indies and the tropical Americas to treat upset stomach, sleeplessness, fatigue, and diarrhea.

# SIMPSON'S STOPPER
*Myrcianthes fragrans* (formerly *Eugenia simpsonii*)

**Also called:** Twinberry, twinberry stopper
**Nativity:** Native
**Florida range:** St. Johns, Alachua, and Hernando Counties discontinuously south through the mainland but mostly in coastal counties
**Habitat:** Hammocks, coastal forests, and shell mounds
**Description:** Tree to 20' tall or more with a smooth, light brown trunk and opposite, ovate, gland-dotted leaves averaging ¾"–1" long and ½"–⅝" wide. White flowers are about ⅜" wide and are followed by fruits that ripen red and measure about ⅜" wide and up to ½" long.
**Comments:** This state-listed threatened species is more common on Long Pine Key in Everglades National Park (Miami-Dade County) than elsewhere in the state where it occurs as a hammock tree or where it is kept shrubby by fire in pine rockland habitat. It is a handsome tree for landscaping and is commonly found in nurseries in South Florida that specialize in native plants.
**Uses:** Ripe fruits can be picked and eaten fresh. In parts of its range in the tropical Americas, a decoction is made by boiling the tender, fragrant branch tips and used to remedy muscle aches and reduce labor pain.

# GUAVA
*Psidium guajava*

**Also called:** *Guayaba* (in Spanish-speaking countries). There are hundreds of cultivar names, but only a few dozen of them are commonly found in cultivation. The red-fruited *Psidium cattleianum* is called cattley guava or strawberry guava, and it is also naturalized in Florida.

**Nativity:** Introduced, with a natural range extending through the West Indies and tropical America

**Florida range:** Throughout the southern half of peninsular Florida into the Florida Keys

**Habitat:** Hammocks, pinelands, coastal strand, and disturbed sites

**Description:** A small tree, usually less than 18" tall but may be taller, with exfoliating bark that creates a smooth trunk. Ovate-elliptic or oblong-elliptic leaves are opposite, averaging 3"–5" long and 2"–3" wide. White flowers are about ½" wide and produce globose (rounded), ovoid (egg-shaped), or pyriform (pear-shaped) fruits that typically ripen yellow and measure 2"–4" long with pink, white, or yellowish pulp. There are numerous cultivated varieties in the nursery trade.

**Cautions:** If you are squeamish, know that the fruits commonly harbor the larvae (maggots) of Caribbean fruit flies. You can consider them added protein, eat them after dark so you don't see them, or pick mature, green, unripe fruits and ripen them at home before the fruit flies lay eggs in them.

**Comments:** To avoid Caribbean fruit flies, commercial growers place paper or mesh bags over unripe fruits so they can ripen inside the bag, which is better than spraying them with systemic insecticides. The ripe fruits of wild, naturalized guavas commonly have larvae inside them. Guava fruits are delicious, so consider yourself lucky if you are out foraging and find fruiting guava trees. However, the yellow-fruited *Psidium guajava* is a listed Category I invasive species in Florida because it invades undisturbed natural habitats and competes with native plants. The red-fruited *Psidium cattleianum* is also a listed Category I invasive species. Raccoons, bears, opossums, and birds spread the seeds, so if you do find wild guavas, pick the fruits and dispose of the seeds so you do not contribute to its spread.

**Uses:** Ripe fruits can be eaten fresh or taken home and used to make jams, compotes, or blended as a fruit punch. Leaves can be dried and brewed into a mild tea, or added as a flavoring when cooking soups or stews. The following recipe from the Caribbean is for a popular beverage called "pog." The name is derived from the first letter of the ingredients—pineapple, orange, guava.

---

## RECIPE

**Pog**

1 ripe guava, peeled and seeded
1 orange, peeled and seeded
¼ fresh pineapple, skinned and cored

Place all ingredients in a blender, fill with ice, and blend on high until smooth. Pour into a glass and enjoy. Adding your favorite rum is optional.

---

# NELUMBONACEAE (LOTUS FAMILY)

## AMERICAN LOTUS
*Nelumbo lutea*

**Also called:** Yellow lotus, water chinquapin, duck acorns
**Nativity:** Native
**Florida range:** From the central Panhandle discontinuously south though the peninsula to Miami-Dade County
**Habitat:** Freshwater lakes, ponds, slow-moving rivers, canals, and sloughs
**Description:** Circular, waterlily-like leaves average about 12" across and usually stand above the water surface. Very showy, yellow flowers appear in spring or early summer and measure 4"–5" wide, exceeding the leaves in height. Seed capsules resemble a showerhead and reach about 4" across, with hard seeds held in pockets.
**Cautions:** American alligators and venomous cottonmouth moccasins share this plant's habitat. It can sometimes be found colonizing roadside canals and grows in much deeper water than waterlilies, so be cautious. When planted in water gardens, the American lotus can be very aggressive, quickly taking over the entire water surface, so much diligence will be required to keep it in check.

**Comments:** The large, tuberous rhizomes of the American lotus were an important starchy carbohydrate in the diet of Native Americans, plus they ate the seeds and young leaves. The pink-flowered sacred lotus (*Nelumbo nucifera*) is native to Asia but has been vouchered as a naturalized species in 4 Florida counties. It is used in traditional Chinese medicine and as food throughout its natural range. Hybrids between the 2 species are in the nursery trade.

**Uses:** Mature root tubers can be washed and baked, and taste similar to the sweet potato, or they can be skinned and chopped as an addition to stews and soups, much like the white potato. They can also be sliced thin and fried like potato chips. Green, immature seeds can be boiled and served like sweet peas, and very young, immature leaves can be boiled until tender and served as a side dish.

# ORCHIDACEAE (ORCHID FAMILY)

## VANILLA ORCHID
*Vanilla planifolia*

**Also called:** Commercial vanilla

**Nativity:** Introduced from the American tropics

**Florida range:** Known to be naturalized in Miami-Dade and Collier Counties, but since it very rarely forms seedpods in Florida without hand-pollination, the wild populations are most likely the result of purposeful introductions.

**Habitat:** Forested swamps and hammocks

**Description:** The stems and leaves of this high-climbing, vining orchid are thick and succulent, with roots that cling to trees, but often climb trees and then hang back down. Thick, fleshy, lanceolate leaves appear at the nodes along with roots that attach to tree trunks as it climbs. The leaves typically reach up to 4"–5" long and 2"–2½" wide. Flowers are green with a yellow inner lip edged in white, and usually require hand-pollinating to produce seedpods.

**Cautions:** The sap from broken stems can cause mild to severe contact dermatitis, so wash your hands with soapy water after contact with the sap, and avoid contact with your eyes.

**Comments:** This familiar orchid is native to Mexico, Guatemala, and Belize, but is cultivated in tropical and subtropical regions by orchid growers and is the principal source of vanilla extract. Madagascar is the leader in vanilla extract production, exporting 80 percent of the global supply. The dried pods of two other species, *Vanilla tahitensis* and *Vanilla pompona* are also sometimes used in vanilla extract production in other parts of the world. Vanilla is second to saffron as being the most expensive spice in the world, because both are labor intensive. This is not a plant to be used by foragers or gardeners immediately upon harvesting the pods, because vanilla extract takes a long time to process, and the pods must be dried first. Because this orchid is uncommon in Florida's wilds, I recommend purchasing plants and growing them at home. You will also need to learn how to hand-pollinate the flowers so seedpods, or "vanilla beans," will be produced. Some orchid nurseries in Florida sell *Vanilla planifolia*, or you can skip growing your own plants and purchase dried pods in grocery stores or order them online. Making your own vanilla extract is surprisingly simple.
**Uses:** Vanilla extract flavoring for baked goods, puddings, and beverages.

## RECIPE

### Vanilla Extract

1 pint bottle of vodka (also try experimenting with rum, brandy, or bourbon)
6 to 8 dried vanilla beans (available for purchase in the spice section of many grocery stores or ordered online)

1. Carefully slice the vanilla beans lengthwise along one side with a sharp knife (some people slice them completely in half and then cut them into 1-inch pieces). Place beans in the bottle of vodka, tighten the lid, and put a label on the bottle with the date.

2. Shake the bottle once a week for at least 4 months, though up to 12 months would be better for maximum flavor. You now have a pint of vanilla extract and saved a whole bunch of money.

# OROBANCHACEAE (BROOMRAPE FAMILY)

## BEACH FALSE FOXGLOVE
*Agalinis fasciculata*

**Also called:** Gerardia (also a former genus name)

**Nativity:** Native

**Florida range:** Throughout all of Florida

**Habitat:** Coastal sands, pinelands, brackish habitats, fields, and disturbed sites

**Description:** Herbaceous annual with branched, ascending, ridged, scabrous stems to 36" tall with leaf blades narrowly to broadly linear, measuring up to 1½" long. Flowers reach 1" wide with 2 parallel cream stripes in the throat surrounded by dark pink dots.

**Cautions:** Be certain to not mistake members of this genus with the unrelated and toxic foxgloves (*Digitalis* spp.), which are widely cultivated for their beautiful flowers that look remarkably similar to false foxgloves (*Agalinis* spp.). *Digitalis* species are not native or naturalized in Florida, but are sometimes cultivated in flower gardens.

**Comments:** There are 17 native *Agalinis* species in Florida, with *Agalinis georgiana* in the Florida Panhandle being the only species listed as state-endangered. All species of *Agalinis* are hemiparasites, parasitizing the roots of nearby plants but also photosynthesizing. The two most common species in Florida are *Agalinis fasciculata* and *Agalinis purpurea*. Flowers on some species look identical, so you will need to rely on leaf characteristics to properly identify them. This species is more partial to disturbed sites than its look-alike, *Agalinis purpurea*.

**Uses:** The dried stems and leaves can be brewed into a tea. Dr. George Hocking (1908–2001), professor emeritus at the College of Pharmacy in Auburn University, noted that in South Carolina, the old stems of this species and *Agalinis purpurea* are boiled in water to "make a nice drink anytime."

# OXALIDACEAE (WOODSORREL FAMILY)

## YELLOW WOODSORREL
*Oxalis corniculata*

**Also called:** Creeping woodsorrel
**Nativity:** Native
**Florida range:** Throughout all of Florida
**Habitat:** Beach dunes, stream banks, fields, open pinelands; a weed of greenhouses, gardens, lawns, and roadsides
**Description:** The leaves of this herbaceous species are divided into 3 rounded leaflets that somewhat resemble an Irish shamrock. The creeping stems root at the nodes, forming extensive colonies. The 5-lobed, yellow flowers reach about ½" wide and produce cylindrical capsules that forcefully eject seeds long distances.
**Cautions:** The leaves are very high in oxalates and should not be eaten if you have a history of kidney stones or other kidney problems. If your doctor has advised you to avoid oxalates in your diet, then scratch all species of *Oxalis* off your edibles list, as well as the related carambola (*Averrhoa carambola*), also called starfruit.

**Comments:** This native species is often found as a weed in lawns and gardens in Florida. The leaves have an interesting sour flavor when eaten. Of the 8 species found in Florida, this species and *Oxalis macrantha* in the Florida Panhandle and Alachua County are considered to be native to Florida. A non-native species with pink flowers, *Oxalis debilis*, is found nearly statewide as a very common lawn and garden weed. The leaves of all species are edible, but read the Cautions section.

**Uses:** The leaves can be picked and eaten or added to salads (see Cautions). Underground tubers produced by some species are edible, especially the non-native *Oxalis tuberosa* that does not occur in Florida. Personally, I avoid eating any species of *Oxalis* due to the high oxalate content in the leaves, but many people eat them with impunity.

# PASSIFLORACEAE (PASSIONFLOWER FAMILY)

Maypop fruit

## MAYPOP
*Passiflora incarnata*

**Also called:** Purple psssionflower
**Nativity:** Native
**Florida range:** Throughout most all of mainland Florida
**Habitat:** Open woodlands, hammock margins, coastal strand, and disturbed sites
**Description:** High-climbing or spreading vine bearing deeply 3-lobed (rarely 5-lobed) leaves with serrate margins, reaching about 5" long and 3½" wide. Showy flowers are up to 3" wide and produce ovoid fruits that measure up to 2" across. The fruits ripen yellow.
**Comments:** This native passionflower is commonly cultivated for its beautiful flowers but also as a larval host plant for zebra longwing, Julia, and gulf fritillary butterflies. It is aggressive in cultivation with a tendency to spread out of bounds by root suckers. It is very closely related to the edible passionfruit, *Passiflora edulis*, and has been used in the nursery trade to create interesting hybrids, such as *Passiflora* x 'Incense' (a cross between *Passiflora incarnata* and *Passiflora cincinnata*), with highly perfumed flowers.
**Uses:** The pulp surrounding the seeds varies in taste from bland to sweet and can be eaten fresh, used to make juice and smoothies, or added to fruit salads. It has numerous historical medicinal uses by Native Americans, including as a sedative and liver tonic, to treat skin infections, and to wean babies off breast-feeding.

## CORKYSTEM PASSIONFLOWER
*Passiflora suberosa (Flora of North America* recognizes *Passiflora pallida)*

**Also called:** *Meloncillo* (in Spanish-speaking countries)
**Nativity:** Native
**Florida range:** Throughout most of peninsular Florida into the Florida Keys
**Habitat:** Pinelands, tropical hardwood hammocks, woodlands, coastal strand, and disturbed sites
**Description:** Small vine with corky outgrowths on mature stems that climbs by tendrils. The alternate leaves vary widely in size and shape, ranging 1"–4" long, and may be linear, lanceolate, lobed on one side or the other, or lobed on both sides. The pale green flowers reach up to ½" wide, bearing round fruits to about ⅜" wide that ripen dark purple.
**Comments:** This quaint little vine is widely cultivated by native-plant enthusiasts, mostly as a larval host plant for zebra longwings, Julia, and gulf fritillary butterflies, which may eat the entire plant to the ground. It can be grown on a fence or allowed to scramble around on shrubs as it does in nature.
**Uses:** The small, round fruits can be picked and eaten fresh.

# PHYTOLACCACEAE (POKEWEED FAMILY)

## POKEWEED
*Phytolacca americana (*formerly *Phytolacca rigida)*

**Also called:** Fat cabbage (Louisiana), poke, crow berry, pigeon berry
**Nativity:** Native
**Florida range:** Throughout all of Florida
**Habitat:** Thickets, woodland borders, canopy gaps, and especially disturbed sites such as pastures, fallow fields, overgrown lots, and roadside ditches
**Description:** Shrubby, herbaceous species up to 10' tall but usually less than half that tall, with red stems when mature. Lanceolate to ovate leaves can reach 10" long and 5" wide, with entire margins. Flowers can be white or greenish white to pinkish and are followed by oval berries to ¾" wide that ripen dark purple to black. Some taxonomists recognize var. *rigida*, with pedicels (fruiting stems) shorter than the berries and erect racemes of flowers.
**Cautions:** Proper preparation and cooking is necessary to remove the toxins. The roots are the most toxic, and symptoms of poisoning include violent vomiting, burning of the mouth, esophagus, and stomach, abdominal cramps, blurred vision, sweating, and convulsions. If you experience any of these symptoms, seek medical assistance. Improper cooking of the

greens (such as steaming instead of boiling in changes of water) may result in explosive diarrhea, so consider yourself duly warned.

**Comments:** Juice from the fruits has been used for ink, as a dye for clothes, and to color wines. Louis XIV of France prohibited the inclusion of pokeweed juice in wines because he said it "injured the flavor," and punishment for getting caught was execution, so he apparently took his wine seriously. Canned pokeweed greens are sold in Louisiana marketplaces, and poke sallet is a traditional Cajun dish (*sallet* is French for salad). Singer-songwriter Tony Joe White wrote and sang a popular hit song in 1968 titled "Poke Salad Annie," which was later sung by Elvis Presley.

**Uses:** To harvest pokeweed leaves, look for the newly sprouted, tender young leaves in spring when the stems are green and tender. Once the plant begins to produce red stems, do not harvest because they become somewhat toxic and bitter at that stage. Also ensure that no portion of the roots is included because they are toxic even when cooked. Regardless of its potential toxicity, pokeweed remains a popular dish in Louisiana's Cajun country as well as in other southern states. For traditional poke sallet, follow the recipe below.

---

RECIPE

**Pokeweed Greens (or Poke Sallet)**

Enough tender young pokeweed leaves and young, green stems to fill a large pot

1. Coarsely chop the tender new leaves and young, green stems.

2. Fill 2 large pots with water and bring the water in both pots to a boil. Add the washed leaves and stems to one pot and boil for about 5 minutes.

3. When done, pour the water off and add the greens to the second pot of boiling water for an additional 3–5 minutes. While cooking, refill the first pot with water and bring to a boil.

4. Drain the leaves and boil a third time for about 2 minutes. It is traditional to add some bacon grease and molasses during the final cooking stage, but this is optional. The leaves should not have any bitter taste at this point and can now be added to cooked beans, omelets, and casseroles, or placed in a bowl and sprinkled with cider vinegar as a side dish.

---

# PINACEAE (PINE FAMILY)

## PINES
*Pinus* spp. *(Pinus densa* pictured)

**Also called:** Pine trees
**Nativity:** Native
**Florida range:** Native pine species are found statewide with differing ranges for each species.
**Habitat:** Pinelands, sandhills, scrub, and coastal strand
**Description:** Straight-trunked trees, branching near the top, with some species reaching 80' tall or more. Narrowly linear leaves are clustered at the branch tips. Brown cones dehisc their seeds in the fall months.
**Cautions:** Avoid species that are not true pines, such as Australian pine (*Casuarina equisetifolia*) and Norfolk Island pine (*Araucaria heterophylla*). Pine sap is very sticky and can permanently stain clothes.

**Comments:** There are 8 native species of pines in Florida, namely sand pine (*Pinus clausa*), yellow pine (*Pinus echinata*), southern slash pine (*Pinus elliottii*), South Florida slash pine (*Pinus densa*), spruce pine (*Pinus glabra*), longleaf pine (*Pinus palustris*), pond pine (*Pinus serotina*), and loblolly pine (*Pinus taeda*). Pine needles are very high in Vitamin C, but when making tea it is important to not allow the water to boil because boiling destroys Vitamin C. I remember a quote from famed forager Euell Gibbons, where he said, "Even parts of the pine are edible."

**Uses:** To make pine needle tea, collect fresh pine needles and cut them with scissors into inch-long pieces until you have enough to fill a 1-cup measuring cup. Add 6 cups water to a stainless-steel pan and bring to a low boil, then reduce the heat to simmer. Add the pine needles and let them steep for 20 minutes. Some like to make stronger tea by removing the pot from the stove, covering the pot with a lid, and letting it sit overnight. Pour through a strainer to remove the needles. If it is too strong, dilute with water. Add honey or sugar as a sweetener, and either make iced tea or reheat it for a pleasing cup of hot tea.

# PLANTAGINACEAE (PLANTAIN FAMILY)

## LEMON BACOPA
*Bacopa caroliniana*

**Also called:** Lemon hyssop, blue waterhyssop
**Nativity:** Native
**Florida range:** Throughout all of Florida except the Florida Keys
**Habitat:** Freshwater marshes, swamps, short-hydroperiod glades, stream margins, ditches, and moist pastures
**Description:** This is a mat-forming herbaceous perennial with leaves that smell like lemon when crushed. Stems are either spreading or ascending to about 6" tall with opposite, sessile, softly hairy leaves that alternate in direction on the stem. The leaves are ovate, to about ⅝" long and up to ½" wide. The ⅜", 5-lobed, bright blue flowers are solitary in the upper leaf axils.
**Cautions:** Because there are medical warnings involving *Bacopa monnieri* (described next), it would be wise to treat this species with the same cautions just to be safe.
**Comments:** This species was used by the Seminole and Miccosukee tribes in Florida as a cough medicine and a sedative. Crushed leaves have a pleasant lemony scent. It is found in areas with reliably wet soil.
**Uses:** The leaves can be picked and eaten fresh, added to salads, or used either fresh or dried to make an enjoyable hot or cold tea with hints of lemon flavor.

# HERB-OF-GRACE
*Bacopa monnieri*

**Also called:** Waterhyssop, brahmi

**Nativity:** Native

**Florida range:** Throughout most of Florida, from the far western Panhandle to the Florida Keys

**Habitat:** Freshwater marshes, wet sands, mudflats, short-hydroperiod glades, and along trails that bisect those habitats

**Description:** Mat-forming herbaceous perennial with succulent, creeping stems that root along the nodes. Succulent, somewhat spatulate leaves reach about ½" long and ¼" wide. The 5-lobed, pale pink or white flowers are about ⅜" wide.

**Cautions:** The leaves are very bitter-tasting. Medical doctors offer precautions and warnings to avoid use when pregnant or breast-feeding, and to also avoid consuming this species if you have a slow heart rate or other heart conditions because it may slow your heart rate. It also may make thyroid conditions, ulcers, and asthma symptoms worse. Just to be on the safe side, it is advisable to consult your physician before taking bacopa in supplement form, or consuming the leaves.

**Comments:** Eating the leaves of this species, or drinking tea made from the dried leaves, requires an acquired taste due to the bitterness, but the mental health benefits more than make up for it. It is also reported that this species supports central nervous system function. It prefers open, sunny habitats with wet soils.

**Uses:** The bitter-tasting leaves can be picked and eaten, added to salads, steamed as a potherb, or dried to brew a bitter tea. It is also sold by pharmacies in supplement form to improve memory, learning capacity, and other mental improvements by having a positive effect on the hippocampus, a complex brain structure located in the temporal lobe that serves a major role in learning ability and memory (see Cautions).

## COMMON PLANTAIN
*Plantago major*

**Also called:** Broadleaf plantain, white-man's footprint (Native Americans), waybread
**Nativity:** Introduced
**Florida range:** Naturalized throughout much of mainland Florida, mostly in disturbed sites
**Habitat:** Typically found colonizing disturbed sites such as roadsides, canal banks, vacant lots, edges of farm fields, groves, and residential landscapes
**Description:** Herbaceous annual with a rosette of broad, elliptical to oval, 3-veined leaves reaching 4"–6" long and 3"–4" wide. Tiny flowers are on erect, unbranched spikes that reach about 6" tall.
**Cautions:** This species is exceptionally weedy, so if you purposely grow it, be prepared to do some weeding, or increase your foraging!
**Comments:** It is believed that this species was one of the first plants to be introduced into North America by European colonists, and Native Americans gave it a name that translated to "white-man's footprint" because it invaded the disturbed soil created by clearing land for British settlements. The leaves are high in carotene and, due to their antiseptic properties, cooked leaves are commonly used in folk medicine and bush medicine as a poultice to treat minor wounds, insect stings, and even venomous snakebites. As a word of advice, if you get bitten by a venomous snake, do not run around looking for plantain leaves—get paramedics to rush you to a hospital as quickly as possible!
**Uses:** Tender young leaves of spring can be picked and eaten or chopped and added to salads, soups, or stews. Older leaves are tough and somewhat stringy but can be finely chopped and boiled in water until soft and served as you would spinach. Also, try baking the leaves: Pick a bunch of plantain leaves, spray them with olive oil and sprinkle with herbs or spices of your choice, then bake on a sheet pan at 350ºF for up to 15 minutes, checking every few minutes to ensure they're not burning. Remove from oven when crispy and serve.

## BROOMWEED
*Scoparia dulcis*

**Also called:** Licoriceweed, bitterbroom

**Nativity:** Native

**Florida range:** Throughout all of mainland Florida

**Habitat:** Moist sandy habitats, flatwoods, and disturbed sites such as citrus groves and roadsides

**Description:** Herbaceous perennial (annual in cold temperate zones) with ascending stems averaging 12"–24" tall with opposite, narrowly oblanceolate or rhombic leaves from ½"–3" long and half as wide. Axillary flowers are white or pink-tinged and measure about ½" wide.

**Cautions:** The tea is used in the tropical Americas as an aphrodisiac, a contraceptive, and an abortifacient without any medical backing, so women attempting to get pregnant, or who are in early stages of pregnancy, should not drink tea made from this species, just to be on the safe side.

**Comments:** A common use of the plant is to bundle the leafy stems together and use them as a broom. It is considered a pantropical weed but is native to the Americas and the West Indies. It is sometimes placed in the Scrophulariaceae (Figwort family).

**Uses:** The leaves are chewed and have an initial bitter taste that then turns sweet, with a flavor somewhat resembling licorice. Tender young leaves can be steamed as a flavorful potherb, and the young leaves are used to sweeten tea in lieu of sugar. Herbal tea brewed from the leaves has a long medicinal history, including for treatment of digestive problems, fever from colds, hypoglycemia, hypertension, diabetes, herpes, anemia, hemorrhoids, diarrhea, and many other ailments. The plant has also been used in treating insect bites and snakebites, with no indication if it works or not.

# POACEAE (GRASS FAMILY)

## TOOTHACHE GRASS
*Ctenium aromaticum*

**Nativity:** Native

**Florida range:** Across the Florida Panhandle south to Highlands, Polk, and Palm Beach Counties

**Habitat:** Pine flatwoods, savannahs, short-hydroperiod prairies, bogs, and other wet to moist habitats, including ecotones between uplands and swampy habitats

**Description:** Perennial grass forming dense tufts (lacking rhizomes) with flat or convolute, aromatic, linear leaves that average 36"–48" tall. There are prominent glands on each side of the leaf midvein. The inflorescence exceeds the upper leaves and bears 2 rows of bristly spikelets.

**Cautions:** Chewing the inflorescence feels like you have a hairy caterpillar in your mouth.

**Comments:** Fatty acid amides (isobutylamides) in the plant are what cause numbing of the mouth when chewed.

**Uses:** Chewing parts of the plant, especially the lower stem and inflorescence, will cause numbing of the mouth and can help relieve toothache when out in the field. This grass could be very handy for hikers who suddenly experience a toothache when they are many miles from a pharmacy or dentist. It's like nature's Novocain. According to *Flora of North America*, the roots are spicy when harvested fresh.

## COMMON REED
*Phragmites berlandieri*

**Also called:** Wild broomcorn, bulrush, reed grass
**Nativity:** Questionably native due to taxonomic confusion
**Florida range:** Throughout much of the Florida Panhandle and from north-central Florida south through peninsular Florida (absent from the northern peninsula and the Florida Keys)
**Habitat:** Freshwater and slightly brackish wetlands, including sloughs, marshes, estuaries, and disturbed areas near high-nutrient input from developments or agriculture
**Description:** A tall, rhizomatous grass that forms extensive colonies in freshwater wetlands with stout stems that reach 12'–16' tall with linear-lanceolate leaves averaging 10"–20" long and ½"–1½" wide. Small flowers are in terminal panicles. Tiny seeds are in narrow, pointed spikelets.
**Cautions:** There are other native and non-native tall grasses that grow in the same habitat. Also, watch for cottonmouth moccasins and American alligators that share its habitat.
**Comments:** This species had been referred to as *Phragmites australis*, which is now regarded by some taxonomists as an introduced European species, and is only known from Pinellas

County in Florida. It has also been called *Phragmites australis* subsp. *berlandieri* and may have spread across the southern United States from Mexico, but *Flora of Florida* regards it as a native species (as *Phragmites berlandieri*). All parts of this grass are edible at certain stages and can be used as raw snacks, cooked greens, condiments, beverages, and as a sweetener. It is the common, tall grass around Anhinga Trail in Everglades National Park.

**Uses:** The young shoots can be harvested and eaten before leaves have formed, and are described as being delicious. Freshly emerged leaves can be harvested and cooked as a potherb, and the roots can be eaten raw or boiled. Dried young leaves are ground into a powder and added to cereals as extra protein, and the seeds can be ground into a flour for thickening gravy or as a coating for fried fish and meats. A sugary gum from the stems has a sweet, licorice-like flavor and can be rolled into balls and eaten as a sweet snack. Also, a powder from ground, mature stems can be moistened and rolled into balls, then cooked over an open fire, similar to roasting marshmallows. Try adding a layer of chocolate and sandwiching it between two pieces of graham crackers for a campfire treat like smores. Native Americans used the stems for arrow shafts, floor mats, ceremonial objects, and musical instruments, and even stuffed the hollow stems with tobacco and smoked them like cigarettes.

# POLYGONACEAE (BUCKWHEAT FAMILY)

## SEAGRAPE
*Coccoloba uvifera*

**Nativity:** Native

**Florida range:** Vouchered from Duval and Flagler Counties south along both coasts into the Florida Keys

**Habitat:** Beach dunes, coastal strand, and rocky shorelines

**Description:** Dioecious tree to 24' tall or more with widely spreading branches and round, red-veined leaves to about 6" long and wide. Flowers are on spikes to 6" long, and females bear round, purple fruits about ½" wide.

**Cautions:** If you are planting a female seagrape as a landscape tree, keep it away from walkways, driveways, and sidewalks because the fruits can stain concrete and cause slip-and-fall accidents. Also note that the seagrape is protected under Florida Statute 161.142, which states that it is unlawful for any purpose to cut, harvest, remove, or eradicate any part of the seagrape tree from any public land or from any private land without consent of the owner of such land.

**Comments:** This is a very popular, handsome, salt-tolerant native tree for coastal landscaping and is sometimes pruned as a dense barrier hedge. The wood from mature trees is used to make attractive bowls and other objects. Extracts from the leaves have been prescribed by doctors to control blood sugar levels in diabetics. Beekeepers place honeybee hives near seagrape trees to produce the popular seagrape honey for marketplaces. The related pigeonplum (*Coccoloba diversifolia*) also occurs in Florida, but the fruits are best described as survival food.

**Uses:** The fully ripe (purple) fruits from female seagrape trees can be picked and eaten fresh or used to make seagrape jelly, wine, syrup, and even vinegar. The following recipe is from my grandmother, Olive Postle, written on a 3x5 card in pencil back in the 1930s.

## RECIPE

### Granny's Seagrape Jelly

8 cups ripe seagrape fruits
4 cups water
1 (1.75-ounce) packet of pectin
¼ cup lemon or lime juice
½ teaspoon butter or margarine
4 cups granulated sugar
8 sterilized 8-ounce canning jars and a roll of cheesecloth

1. Wash seagrapes in a colander and remove any unripe fruits.

2. Place the seagrapes and 4 cups of water (or enough water to cover) in a stainless-steel pot and cook over medium heat for 1–1½ hours until the skin softens and the seeds begin to separate from the fruits. Use a potato masher to help separate the seeds and skin from the fruits.

3. Pour the mixture through a colander into a bowl, pressing the seagrapes to remove as much liquid as possible. Place cheesecloth over another large bowl and pour the mixture into the cheesecloth before lifting it like a bag and squeezing the liquid through to further separate the liquid from any leftover pulp.

4. Return to the stainless-steel pot and add enough water to bring the total to 5 cups. Bring the seagrape water mixture to a boil and add the pectin, lemon or lime juice, and butter, then stir in the sugar until it dissolves.

5. Pour the mixture into the sterilized canning jars, tighten the lids, and let sit overnight. Refrigerate and enjoy.

## MILD WATERPEPPER
*Persicaria hydropiperoides (*formerly *Polygonum hydropiperoides)*

**Also called:** Swamp smartweed
**Nativity:** Native
**Florida range:** Throughout all of mainland Florida (absent from the Florida Keys)
**Habitat:** Damp soils, ditches, stream banks, pond and lake margins, and wet depressions
**Description:** Herbaceous perennial with tubelike sheaths along the stem above the leaf bases and narrowly lanceolate leaves measuring 1½"–4" long and ¼"–½" wide. Small, white to pinkish, ⅛" flowers are on jointed stalks with 4–6 petal-like sepals.
**Cautions:** Juice from the stems can cause irritation of the eyes.
**Comments:** The names smartweed and waterpepper both refer to the acrid or burning taste of the leaves, although this species is milder than other members of the genus. There are numerous medicinal uses bestowed upon smartweeds, including as treatments for cholera, rheumatism, toothaches, epilepsy, gangrene, and diarrhea, but without any medical backing. Studies with animals have shown that members of this genus have contraceptive properties.
**Uses:** The leaves of smartweeds have been used as a seasoning for foods since ancient times, so try them chopped in salads or added to steamed vegetable dishes.

# FLORIDA DOCK
## *Rumex floridanus*

**Also called:** Water dock, water sorrel, swamp dock
**Nativity:** Native
**Florida range:** Throughout most of mainland Florida (absent in the Florida Keys)
**Habitat:** Freshwater swamps, lake margins, ponds, ditches, shallow canals, streams, and river banks
**Description:** Herbaceous, wetland perennial with erect or reclining stems and broadly lan-ceolate, fleshy leaves reaching 8"–10" long and about 1½"– 2" wide, sometimes with a red midvein. Branched inflorescences are terminal or axillary with small, creamy white flowers in whorls. The seeds (achenes) are brown to dark brown.
**Cautions:** Gather only the young leaves because old leaves become bitter. Medical studies have shown that species of dock have laxative effects.
**Comments:** This is the most widespread species of *Rumex* in Florida. Of the 11 species in Florida, only 2 are native to the state, but all are edible. Dock leaves do not cook down like other greens, so a smaller number of leaves will fill a bowl after cooking than with other greens. *Flora of North America* and *Flora of the Southeastern United States* (Weakley et al.,

2022) refer to this species as *Rumex floridanus*, while *Flora of Florida* refers to it as *Rumex verticillatus*, so take your pick.

**Uses:** Dock leaves are widely eaten around the world, but they are better known for their medicinal uses to treat scorpion stings and burning caused by nettles, ward off smallpox and jaundice, treat liver and intestinal disorders, relieve menstrual problems, and as a laxative tonic. As a potherb, simply harvest fresh young leaves and boil them as you would any green, but remove them from the first pot after boiling for about 5 minutes and add them to a second pot of boiling water and continue cooking to reduce some of the bitter flavor. Try sprinkling the cooked greens with cider vinegar before serving.

# PONTEDERIACEAE (PICKERELWEED FAMILY)

## WATER HYACINTH
*Eichhornia crassipes*

**Also called:** Some botanists refer to this plant as *Pontederia crassipes*.
**Nativity:** Introduced from South America
**Florida range:** Statewide except for the Florida Keys
**Habitat:** Freshwater ponds, lakes, streams, rivers, canals, and other bodies of freshwater
**Description:** Floating herbaceous species with swollen, spongy petioles and rounded leaves reaching 3"–4" wide connected to dense clusters of black roots below the water surface. Showy flowers are pale violet with an upper petal bearing purple lines around a yellow blotch.
**Cautions:** It is reported that eating the flowers or leaves raw may cause itching. This aquatic species occurs in American alligator and cottonmouth moccasin habitat, so be aware.
**Comments:** Some botanists believe that the genus *Eichhornia* belongs as a synonym of *Pontederia* and that this species should be *Pontederia crassipes*. In *Flora of the Southeastern United States* (Weakley et al., 2022), it has been relegated as *Oshuna crassipes*, and is

considered to be a monotypic genus. By whatever name you want to call it, it still tastes the same. Many authorities regard water hyacinth as the worst weed in the world because it can multiply vegetatively very rapidly, producing 3,000 new plants in less than 2 months, and is capable of covering the entire surface of ponds, lakes, slow-moving rivers, and canals if left unchecked, cutting off surface-to-air contact and impeding recreational activities. Although water hyacinth is available for sale on the internet, it is prohibited to cultivate in Alabama, Arkansas, California, Florida, Louisiana, South Carolina, and Texas.

**Uses:** The inflated leaf bases can be deep-fried in oil and have been described as being "crisp like pork rind or popcorn." Dr. Julia Morton (1912–1996) wrote that "young leaves, leafstalks, and flower clusters may be thoroughly cooked and eaten." She did not elaborate on the cooking method, but I would assume it is by boiling in water.

# PICKERELWEED
*Pontederia cordata*

**Also called:** Wampee, pikeweed
**Nativity:** Native
**Florida range:** Throughout all of Florida
**Habitat:** Freshwater wetlands, including sloughs, swamps, ditches, canal banks, and shorelines of streams, rivers, lakes, and springs
**Description:** Rhizomatous, herbaceous perennial averaging 12"–30" tall with linear-lanceolate to somewhat arrow-shaped leaf blades averaging 6"–8" long and 2"–4" wide on long, fleshy petioles. Spikes of ⅜", blue (rarely white) flowers typically overtop the leaves.
**Cautions:** This wetland species occurs in American alligator and cottonmouth moccasin habitat, so be aware.
**Comments:** This common freshwater wetland species should be familiar to most Floridians, often seen flowering in ditches and canal banks adjacent to roadways. It is a superb butterfly attractor but seldom cultivated because it requires permanently wet soil.
**Uses:** The seeds can be ground into flour for baking bread, harvested and eaten fresh (especially when immature), or boiled and eaten as a breakfast cereal.

# PORTULACACEAE (PURSLANE FAMILY)

## FIELD PURSLANE
*Portulaca oleracea*

**Also called:** Hogweed, pigweed, pusley

**Nativity:** Considered native to Florida by most taxonomists, but it has been suggested that it may have originated in Africa and later spread around the world—another one of nature's mysteries.

**Florida range:** Throughout all of Florida

**Habitat:** Typically found in disturbed sites, such as groves, pastures, agricultural fields, roadsides, trail margins, canal banks, and residential landscapes; occasionally found on beach dunes

**Description:** Herbaceous annual or short-lived perennial with spreading or ascending fleshy stems and flattened, obovate or spatulate leaves. The leaves and stems can be green or red, averaging ⅜"–⅝" long and ¼"–⅜" wide. The yellow flowers are about ⅜" across.

**Cautions:** Purslanes contain oxalates and, when eaten in quantity, can be a health issue for people who are prone to kidney stones. Consuming the leaves triggers a toxic reaction in cats.

**Comments:** Not only are the leaves high in vitamins and important minerals, but they contain the richest source of an omega-3 fatty acid, called alpha-linolenic acid, of any leafy vegetable studied to date. The plant is used medicinally to treat cardiovascular disease and is fed to chickens to reduce cholesterol in eggs. One study placed this species in the top 10 worst weeds in the world, yet it is highly cherished as a nutritional vegetable in tropical and temperate regions worldwide.

**Uses:** The leaves can be eaten fresh, added to salads, cooked as a potherb, or lightly sautéed in a pan as a side dish. In parts of Mexico, cooked leaves are added to the filling for tacos and burritos. In Argentina the leaves are used as a base to make a tasty and healthful chimichurri that is used as a condiment with chicken, fish, pork, or vegetable dishes. The leaves are used to thicken dishes such as soups and stews, and as a garnish for egg omelets and meat dishes. In France, the leaves are used as a flavoring in bearnaise sauce.

## RECIPE

**Pickled Purslane**

¼ pound washed purslane leaves
3 fresh fronds of dill
1 fresh or dried tabasco pepper
1 garlic clove, crushed
1½ cups white wine vinegar
1½ cups water
1 teaspoon salt
½ teaspoon dill seeds
½ teaspoon coriander seeds
¼ teaspoon fennel seeds
¼ teaspoon black pepper
¼ teaspoon allspice

1. Put the purslane leaves, dill fronds, tabasco pepper, and garlic into a sterilized quart mason jar.

2. Combine the remaining ingredients in a stainless-steel pan and bring to a boil. Pour liquid into the jar with the purslane leaves and spices, then screw the cap on. Allow to cool before storing in the refrigerator.

3. Serve as a side dish or as a snack to nibble on.

## RECIPE

**Purslane Chimichurri**

1 cup washed purslane leaves
1 cup parsley leaves
1 tablespoon dried oregano or marjoram
3 garlic cloves, smashed and chopped
1 teaspoon crushed red pepper or 1 whole jalapeño, chopped
½ cup olive oil
2 tablespoons red wine vinegar
Salt and freshly ground pepper to taste

Place all ingredients in a blender or food processor and blend until smooth. It is now ready to use as a condiment. Enjoy!

# PTERIDACEAE (MAIDENHAIR FERN FAMILY)

## LEATHER FERN
*Acrostichum danaeifolium*

**Also called:** Giant leather fern
**Nativity:** Native
**Florida range:** From Dixie, Marion, and St. Johns Counties continuously south through the Florida Keys
**Habitat:** Freshwater marshes, swamps, wet hammocks, tree islands, ditches, and canal banks
**Description:** This is a robust fern with large fronds that can reach 6 feet long. Another similar species is coastal leather fern (*Acrostichum aureum*), a state-listed threatened species found in coastal strand and mangrove habitats. A key difference between the two species is that all of the pinnae (leaflets) on *Acrostichum danaeifolium* become fertile and produce spores, while only the pinnae near the tip of the fronds on *A. aureum* will become fertile. Otherwise, the two species look practically identical, but they each have different habitat preferences. The fiddleheads are fronds that have not yet unfurled, and can be found in the center of the rosette of leaves. If a fiddlehead is removed, the plant will simply produce another one, so

harvesting fiddleheads does not harm the plant. This is the largest fern species in Florida, so the fiddleheads are much larger than on other native ferns.

**Uses:** The fiddleheads can be eaten raw, chopped and added to salads, steamed, or dipped in batter and fried. Eaten raw, the fiddleheads are somewhat mucilaginous, similar to raw okra, and have a flavor somewhat like raw asparagus. The fresh, young leaves that have just begun to unfurl can be chopped, steamed, and served as a side dish. Seminoles chopped the young leaves and fiddleheads, soaked them in water, and used it as a skin wash to reduce high fevers, but there is no medical research to prove its effectiveness.

---

RECIPE

**Sautéed Leather Fern Fiddleheads**

8–10 young fiddleheads, washed and cleaned of any brown papery skin
1 tablespoon olive oil
2 tablespoons plant-based butter (or regular butter)
2 cloves garlic, crushed and diced
1 tablespoon lemon juice
1 teaspoon lemon zest

1. Chop the fiddleheads into bite-size pieces.

Sautéed leather fern fiddleheads

2. Bring a large, stainless-steel pot of water to a boil and cook the chopped fiddleheads for about 15 minutes. Drain and rinse them in a strainer.

3. Heat the olive oil and 1 tablespoon of the butter in a large pan over medium heat. Add the garlic and fiddleheads and cook for 5 minutes, stirring occasionally.

4. Stir in the remaining butter plus the lemon juice and lemon zest. Cook for another 3 minutes over high heat, stirring frequently.

5. Serve as a side dish.

# RHAMNACEAE (BUCKTHORN FAMILY)

## SOLDIERWOOD
*Colubrina elliptica*

**Also called:** Mauby (West Indies)

**Nativity:** Native

**Florida range:** Florida Keys (Miami-Dade and Monroe Counties)

**Habitat:** Tropical hardwood hammocks of the Florida Keys

**Description:** Tree to about 25' tall with exfoliating bark that peels off in strips. Alternate, elliptic leaves average 2½"–3½" long and 1½"–2" wide. Green, star-shaped, ¼" flowers are congested in the leaf axils. The fruits are orange red with tiny, glossy, black seeds.

**Cautions:** If you live in the Florida Keys, be aware that poisonwood (*Metopium toxiferum*) also has bark that peels off in strips, so be certain of your identification (see the Poisonous Plants chapter in this guide).

**Comments:** This native tree occurs in the West Indies (including the Bahamas) and into tropical America, but in Florida it only occurs naturally in the forests of the Florida Keys. Nurseries in South Florida that specialize in Florida native plants may offer this tree for sale.

It is not really a tree to stop and forage on, but is included in this guide because it is the source of a very popular tea in the West Indies.

**Uses:** The exfoliating bark is used as a key ingredient in mauby tea. In the Miami area there are local Caribbean groceries that sell mauby bark, or you can order it on the internet, which is also where you can find numerous recipes and instructional videos on making your own mauby tea. A basic recipe is offered here.

## RECIPE

**Mauby Tea**

6–8 pieces of mauby (soldierwood bark), each about 4 inches long
2 cinnamon sticks
2 pieces of star anise
10 whole cloves or several more cinnamon sticks (depending on your taste preference)
2 bay leaves
1 tablespoon anise seed

1. Boil all ingredients in 3 or 4 cups of water for 20 minutes. Remove from heat and let cool.

2. When cooled, pour the concentrate into a bowl and add 10 cups of water. Sweeten with brown sugar or dark honey and then strain into a bowl and refrigerate. If it is too bitter-tasting, add more water and sugar.

*Note:* Some recipes call for 1 teaspoon vanilla extract, dried orange peel, and/or ginger as ingredients, so feel free to experiment.

Mauby tea ingredients

Mauby tea

## CHEWSTICK
*Gouania lupuloides*

**Also called:** Whiteroot

**Nativity:** Native

**Florida range:** Vouchered from Clay, Brevard, Indian River, Manatee, Martin, and Miami-Dade Counties and the Monroe County mainland and Keys

**Habitat:** Margins of hardwood forests, fencerows, and edges of clearings

**Description:** Small, somewhat woody vine, climbing with tendrils or scrambling, and bearing alternate, elliptic, ovate, or lanceolate leaves with hairy petioles and serrate margins. The leaves average 1½"–2½" long and ½"–1" wide. Small, white flowers are borne in axillary or terminal racemes. Fruits break into 3 2-winged samaras.

**Cautions:** The vine contains saponins that create a bitter, soapy taste.

**Comments:** When the end of a piece of mature stem is chewed, it frays and the saponins in the stem create a soapy, aromatic, and bitter taste. Once chewed, the frayed stem is used as a toothbrush, especially in the West Indies, Mexico, and Central America.

**Uses:** Mature stems can be cut off and chewed on one end to create a makeshift toothbrush used to clean your teeth and harden your gums. In Central America, ash from burned leaves is used to speed healing of body sores. In Jamaica the leaves are used in place of hops to brew beer.

# BLACK IRONWOOD
*Krugiodendron ferreum*

**Also called:** Leadwood
**Nativity:** Native
**Florida range:** From Brevard County south along the east coast to Miami-Dade County and the Monroe County mainland into the Monroe County Keys
**Habitat:** Hardwood hammocks
**Description:** Tropical hardwood tree to 30' tall with opposite, glossy, ovate to elliptic leaves that are notched at the tip and average 1"–1½" long and ¾" wide. Flowers are somewhat star-shaped, green, and measure about ¼" across, followed by round, ¼" fruits that ripen black.
**Cautions:** A decoction made from the roots is said to be purgative.
**Comments:** The wood of this species is regarded as the heaviest in the United States, weighing 89 pounds per cubic foot.
**Uses:** Although they are small, the ripe, black fruits can be eaten fresh and are quite sweet and tasty.

## DARLING PLUM
*Reynosia septentrionalis*

**Also called:** Red ironwood

**Nativity:** Native

**Florida range:** Miami-Dade County and Monroe County Keys

**Habitat:** Tropical hardwood hammocks

**Description:** Small tree to about 20' tall with leathery, elliptic-oblong to obovate leaves, averaging 1" long and ½" wide with a blunt, notched tip. Green flowers are 4-lobed and reach about ¼" wide, followed by dark purple to black, globose to ellipsoid fruits. The fruits are drupes, and produce a single, hard seed.

**Cautions:** This is a state-listed threatened species, so if you find fruiting trees where it is legal to harvest, leave the seeds behind so they have a chance to germinate.

**Comments:** This tropical tree is only known from the Florida Keys (Miami-Dade and Monroe Counties). Rather than harvesting seeds from wild trees, even where it may be legal to forage, it would be preferable to purchase trees in a local nursery and grow them as landscape trees so you can forage right from your own garden.

**Uses:** The ripe fruits can be picked and eaten and have a pleasantly sweet flavor, although there is very little pulp around the seeds. Mature trees can produce hundreds of fruits, so if you have them in quantity, they can be boiled to separate the seeds and skin from the pulp. Strain the mixture, add sugar to taste, and boil until thickened to make a pleasant-tasting syrup.

# ROSACEAE (ROSE FAMILY)

## VIRGINIA STRAWBERRY
*Fragaria virginiana*

**Also called:** Wild strawberry

**Nativity:** Native

**Florida range:** Vouchered from Jackson and Leon Counties in Florida's central Panhandle but more common across much of the United States into Canada

**Habitat:** Openings in woodlands, prairies, limestone glades, meadows, and roadsides

**Description:** Stoloniferous perennial with trifoliate leaves on long, hairy petioles. The obovate to elliptic-obovate, toothed leaflets measure ¾"–2" long and ½"–1¼" wide. The white, 5-petaled flowers measure 1"–1¼" across and are followed by clusters of small strawberries that ripen red.

**Cautions:** The fruits are so tasty you may eat way too many of them!

**Comments:** The Virginia strawberry was hybridized with two other species to produce the strawberries of commerce. It often grows in patches in open fields with well-drained soils. Because this species has a very limited range in Florida, it would be a prime candidate for cultivation so you can harvest fruits from your own garden. Check native-plant nurseries located in the Florida Panhandle.

**Uses:** Fresh, ripe fruits can be picked and eaten, added to fruit salads or breakfast cereal, used as a decorative topping on vanilla or strawberry ice cream, or added to a blender with milk to make a smoothie. If you are lucky enough to have an abundance of fruits, they can be used to make pies.

## CHICKASAW PLUM
*Prunus angustifolia*

**Also called:** Cherokee plum, Florida sand plum, sandhill plum
**Nativity:** Native
**Florida range:** Across much of the Florida Panhandle and the northern peninsula south to Hillsborough, Lake, and Volusia Counties
**Habitat:** Xeric woodlands, pastures, fencerows, and dry, open sites
**Description:** Deciduous, thorny shrub up to 12' tall, often forming clonal colonies, or occasionally a tree to 30' tall. As a shrub, it is often as wide as it is tall. Alternate, lanceolate leaves average 1½"–3" long and half as wide, with bluntly toothed (crenulate-serrulate) margins with conspicuous reddish-orange glands. White, fragrant, 5-petaled flowers are produced in mass each spring and are followed by ½"–1" edible fruits that change color from green to red to yellow as they ripen.
**Cautions:** Along with many other species of moths, the leaves are fed upon by the larvae of the io moth (*Automeris io*), which is covered with stinging hairs. The bristly caterpillar is green with a red-and-white stripe running horizontally down each side. Touching one will cause an immediate burning pain, much like a wasp sting. If you get stung, place tape over the affected area and pull it off to remove the bristles, then wipe the area with ammonia.
**Comments:** Chickasaw plum commonly hybridizes with other species of *Prunus*, but no hybrids have been recognized and vouchered in Florida.
**Uses:** Ripe fruits can be picked and eaten, made into jellies, or used to make pies and other desserts.

## ALLEGHENY PLUM
*Prunus umbellata*

**Also called:** Flatwoods plum, hog plum, sloe
**Nativity:** Native
**Florida range:** Across the Florida Panhandle and the northern peninsula south to Sarasota, DeSoto, Highlands, and Martin Counties
**Habitat:** Mixed pine-hardwoods, pine flatwoods, xeric forests, coastal scrub, and sandhills
**Description:** Moderately thorny, deciduous shrub or small tree 10'–20' tall bearing hairy, elliptic to broadly elliptic leaves that measure 1½"–3" long and ½"–1½" wide, toothed along the margins. White (sometimes turning pink), 5-petaled flowers appear before or during leaf emergence in springtime. Fruits (drupes) measure about ½" wide and may be red, yellow, purple, or nearly black.
**Cautions:** The cautions for Chickasaw plum, described previously, also apply to this species.
**Comments:** Note that the alternate common name, hog plum, is more commonly used for *Ximenia americana*, also included in this guide. The name sloe also applies to other *Prunus* species, especially a European species used to make a gin-based liqueur called sloe gin.
**Uses:** Ripe fruits can be picked and eaten, made into jellies, or used to make pies and other desserts.

## RECIPE

**Allegheny Plum Sloe Gin**
(alcoholic)

1 pound ripe Allegheny plum fruits
½ pound granulated sugar
1 fifth (750 ml.) white gin

1. Pierce each cleaned and dried plum with a fork.

2. Place the plums in a 2-quart sealable jar. Add the sugar and gin and seal the lid. Shake well and then shake the jar once or twice a day for at least 7 days.

3. Place a label on the jar with the date and store in a cool, dry place for 3 months.

4. Strain the liquid through muslin or a coffee filter into a large bowl. Discard the plums.

5. Pour into clean bottles, seal, and label.

**Note:** Although the sloe gin is now ready to drink, it will improve with age, and allowing it to age for a year will greatly improve the flavor. The key is to make the gin one year to drink the following year. Cheers!

# SOUTHERN DEWBERRY
*Rubus trivialis*

**Also called:** Southern blackberry
**Nativity:** Native
**Florida range:** Throughout Florida except Miami-Dade and Monroe Counties (mainland and Keys)
**Habitat:** Open fields, borders of marshes, marshy swales, roadsides, and fencerows
**Description:** The branches and flower stems of this sprawling species are armed with sharp, recurved thorns and coarse, glandular hairs. The compound leaves bear 3–5 leaflets that are mostly elliptic to narrowly ovate with toothed margins. Solitary flowers are white (rarely pinkish) and measure about 1" wide. Oblong fruits ripen black.
**Cautions:** Wickedly sharp, recurved thorns line the stems.
**Comments:** Sand blackberry (*Rubus cuneifolius*), northern dewberry (*Rubus flagellaris*), and sawtooth blackberry (*Rubus pensilvanicus*) are also native to Florida. Lucky you if you find any of the native blackberries with ripe fruits while out hiking. Remember to leave plenty for the bears, raccoons, gopher tortoises, and other wildlife.
**Uses:** The delicious ripe fruits can be picked and eaten fresh, used in pies, and added to fruit salads, cereal, yogurt, or any other dishes where you would normally use store-bought blackberries.

## Southern Dewberry Pie

4 cups dewberries, washed
½ cup granulated sugar
½ cup all-purpose flour
1 pre-made 9-inch double pie crust (or make your own)
2 tablespoons milk

1. Preheat oven to 425ºF.

2. Combine dewberries with sugar and flour in a large bowl.

3. Place bottom pie crust in a pie pan. Pour mixture into the bottom pie crust. Cover with the top crust and cut several slits in the center to allow steam to escape. Brush the top pie crust with milk.

4. Bake pie in the preheated 425ºF oven for 15 minutes, then reduce heat to 375ºF for 20 minutes, or until crust is golden brown. Remove from oven and cool.

5. For even more decadence, serve slices topped with vanilla ice cream.

# RUBIACEAE (MADDER FAMILY)

## SEVEN-YEAR APPLE
*Casasia clusiifolia (*formerly *Genipa clusiifolia)*

**Also called:** Jenipapo (South America)
**Nativity:** Native
**Florida range:** Coastal forests of Lee, Collier, Broward, Miami-Dade, and Monroe Counties, including the Florida Keys
**Habitat:** Coastal scrub and hammocks
**Description:** Dioecious shrub or small tree to about 10' tall with opposite, dark green, glossy, obovate leaves from 3½"–5" long and 2"–3" wide, rounded at the tip. Male flowers are in axillary clusters, with flowers on females usually solitary. Ovoid to obovoid fruits reach 3" long and 1¾" wide, ripening from green to black. The pulp is black.
**Cautions:** The sap can stain skin and clothing.
**Comments:** The sap contains genipin, which turns black when it comes into contact with skin, so a principal use of the sap by indigenous tribes in tropical America was for body painting.
**Uses:** The black, wrinkled, ripe fruits can be punctured and the contents squeezed or sucked into your mouth. Some have said it has a licorice flavor, but Dr. Dan Austin (1943–2015) considered the flavor to be disgusting. Try it, though, you might like it!

# WILD COFFEE
*Psychotria nervosa*

**Also called:** Seminole balsamo

**Nativity:** Native

**Florida range:** Throughout peninsular Florida into the Florida Keys

**Habitat:** Hardwood hammocks, pinelands, and coastal strand; a common hammock understory species in South Florida

**Description:** Woody shrub reaching up to 10' tall but typically to about 6' in height. Glossy, dark green, narrowly obovate leaves are typically about 3" long and 2" wide with prominently raised veins. Small, white flowers are in terminal clusters and are followed by oval, ¼" fruits that ripen red.

**Cautions:** Reports of the seeds being hallucinogenic are not backed by scientific or medical research.

**Comments:** There are two other species of wild coffee native to Florida—*Psychotria tenuifolia* occurs throughout the central and southern Florida mainland, and *Psychotria ligustrifolia* is restricted to Miami-Dade County and the Florida Keys. The non-native *Psychotria punctata* is naturalized in Miami-Dade County and the Florida Keys. The name wild coffee relates to these shrubs being related to true coffee (*Coffea arabica*), but the seeds of wild coffee do not contain caffeine. Coffee-like beverages brewed from wild coffee seeds reportedly result in a "bad taste and terrible headaches." Wild coffee is commonly cultivated in warmer parts of Florida to attract birds and butterflies.

**Uses:** The attractive red fruits are edible fresh, but they look much better than they taste. Some foragers have described them as sweet, while others regard them as bland. Whether or not you'll eat them with gusto depends on how hungry you are, or how long you've been lost in the woods.

# SAPINDACEAE (SOAPBERRY FAMILY)

## BALLOONVINE
*Cardiospermum corindum*

**Also called:** Faux persil (false parsley)

**Nativity:** Native

**Florida range:** Miami-Dade and Monroe Counties (both mainland and Keys)

**Habitat:** Hammock margins, canopy gaps, and fences

**Description:** Herbaceous perennial vine with ribbed stems that climbs by tendrils and bears compound leaves divided into 3 ovate, coarsely toothed leaflets. The flowers produce balloon-like, angled pods to about 1" wide. Round, hard, black seeds have a white, semicircular hilum.

**Cautions:** A form of soap substitute made by rubbing the leaves in water to release the saponins is known to irritate the skin on some people.

**Comments:** Two other species occur in Florida. Heartseed (*Cardiospermum microcarpum*) is a native species that ranges from the Florida Keys north into Alachua County, and love-in-a-puff (*Cardiospermum halicacabum*) is a non-native species vouchered from Seminole, Brevard, Polk, and Miami-Dade Counties, and the Monroe County Keys. They all look quite similar.

**Uses:** Tender new leaves can be harvested, boiled, and served as a potherb.

## SOAPBERRY
*Sapindus saponaria*

**Also called:** Florida soapberry, wingleaf soapberry, soap tree
**Nativity:** Native
**Florida range:** Lee and Hendry Counties south through the Florida Keys. Trees that occur north of Lee County into the Florida Panhandle are believed to be *Sapindus marginatus*, but the two species look remarkably similar.
**Habitat:** Coastal and inland hammocks
**Description:** Deciduous tree to 40' tall or more with alternate, pinnately compound leaves measuring 8"–20" long with narrowly lanceolate leaflets. The leaf stems are prominently winged. Small, white flowers are in dense, terminal panicles followed by marble-size green fruits that ripen brownish orange.
**Cautions:** The inedible fruits are toxic to eat and have been used to poison fish in shallow water. Sensitive people may develop a skin rash from handling crushed fruits due to the high saponin content.
**Comments:** Although this is not a tree with edible fruits for foragers, the fruits are widely used throughout its natural range in the Caribbean and the American tropics as a source of soap for laundering clothes. The fruits reportedly contain up to 37 percent saponin, a key ingredient in soap products. There will not be a lot of suds like in commercial laundry detergents, but it is much more environmentally friendly due to the lack of chemicals and

artificial fragrances. Some taxonomists choose to recognize the similar-looking trees in central and northern Florida as a separate species (*Sapindus marginatus*).

**Uses:** Make a detergent to wash clothes, or as a body wash and hair shampoo for you (see Cautions) and your dog, or to spray on plants as a non-toxic way to control aphids, mealybugs, and other soft-bodied insects.

RECIPE

**Soapberry Detergent**

15–20 whole, ripe soapberry fruits
6 cups water

1. Pour water into a stainless-steel pot. Add soapberry fruits and bring the water to a boil. Reduce heat to low and simmer for 20–30 minutes.

2. Strain the liquid into a bowl and let cool.

3. It is best to keep the liquid in the refrigerator. For long-term storage, fill ice cube trays with the liquid and place in the freezer.

4. For washing a normal load of clothes, add ½ cup liquid or several ice cubes (thawing first is not necessary) of soapberry detergent to the washer.

# SAPOTACEAE (SAPODILLA FAMILY)

## WILD DILLY
*Manilkara jaimiqui* subsp. *emarginata*

**Also called:** Dilly

**Nativity:** Native

**Florida range:** Collier and Miami-Dade Counties and the Monroe County Keys

**Habitat:** Coastal scrub, tropical hardwood hammocks, and rocky shorelines

**Description:** Tree to 18' tall but typically much shorter. Oblong-elliptic leaves are notched at the tip and measure 1½"–4" long and ¾"–1½" wide. Axillary, greenish-yellow, ⅜" flowers have 6 hairy sepals and 6 lobes. Brown, oval fruits reach 1¼" wide.

**Cautions:** The white latex from unripe fruits can make your fingers very sticky. The fruits should be eaten in moderation to avoid constipation.

**Comments:** This is a state-listed threatened species that is mostly found within state parks in the Florida Keys where it is illegal to forage. Foragers in southern Florida are encouraged to purchase trees in local nurseries that specialize in Florida native plants and add this tree to your landscape.

**Uses:** Like the related non-native sapodilla, the fully ripe fruits can be peeled and eaten fresh.

Sapodilla fruits

# SAPODILLA
*Manilkara zapota*

**Also called:** Dilly, sapote, gum elemi
**Nativity:** Introduced
**Florida range:** Vouchered from Lee and Palm Beach Counties south into the Monroe County Keys
**Habitat:** Invasive in hardwood hammocks, especially in the Florida Keys
**Description:** Large tree to 50' tall or more with a dense canopy of elliptic to ovate, dark green, glossy leaves averaging about 4" long and 2"–2½" wide. Small, bell-like flowers are white. Round to slightly oblong fruits are brown and measure 2"–3" wide with pulp that ranges from pale yellow to pale orangish brown. Seeds are dark brown.
**Cautions:** The white latex from the unripe fruits and inner bark can make your fingers very sticky. This is a Category I invasive species listed by the Florida Invasive Species Council. If you find wild trees and choose to eat the fruits, carry the seeds out with you so you do not contribute to its spread.
**Comments:** The latex contains chicle and is used to make chewing gum. If you dribble some latex from an unripe fruit into the palm of your hand and then stir it with a finger, it will magically turn into a form of gum. Chicle was even chewed by the Aztecs in ancient times. Sapodilla fruits can sometimes be found in local South Florida markets.
**Uses:** Ripe fruits on the ground can be peeled and eaten, and the malty flavor somewhat resembles a pear mixed with brown sugar. Fully mature fruits on the tree can be picked and allowed to ripen at home. Eat them in moderation to avoid constipation.

# FALSE MASTIC
*Sideroxylon foetidissimum (*formerly *Mastichodendron foetidissimum)*

**Also called:** Mastic, yellow mastic

**Nativity:** Native

**Florida range:** From Volusia and Manatee Counties south along both coasts into the Florida Keys

**Habitat:** Hammocks

**Description:** Large tree to 80' tall or more, often with a buttressed trunk with bark that breaks off in thick, squarish patches. Leaves are lanceolate, averaging 4"–5" long and 1"–1½" wide, typically with wavy margins. Yellow, somewhat ill-smelling, ¼" flowers are crowded along the branches and are followed by oblong, yellow to yellow-orange fruits that average about 1¼" long and half as wide.

**Cautions:** Unripe fruits have very sticky latex.

**Comments:** False mastic is most common in the tropi-cal hardwood hammocks of the southeastern mainland, where it can reach more than 100' tall. The species name refers to the fetid-smelling flowers, but overripe fruits lying en masse beneath mature trees smell funky, too. Numerous mammals feed on the fruits, as do birds that pick at the flesh. The flowers attract an array of insects, which in turn attract birds.

**Uses:** Fully ripe fruits can be picked and eaten. Trees are harvested in the West Indies as a favored wood for ship building.

# SCROPHULARIACEAE (FIGWORT FAMILY)

## GOATWEED
*Capraria biflora*

**Also called:** Mexican tea, Jamaican tea, West Indian tea
**Nativity:** Native
**Florida range:** Lee and Martin Counties south throughout the southern Florida mainland into the Florida Keys
**Habitat:** Pinelands, coastal strand, shell mounds, hammock margins, and disturbed sites
**Description:** Herbaceous subshrub to 6' tall or less, usually much branched, with alternate, oblanceolate, toothed leaves averaging 1"–2" long and ½"–¾" wide. Axillary flowers are on long stems, often paired, and measure about ½" wide.
**Cautions:** The roots contain antibiotic alkaloids that, if taken in large doses, can cause dizziness.
**Comments:** Goatweed is often used as a medicinal tea to treat a long list of maladies, including colds, coughs, diabetes, diarrhea, gonorrhea, indigestion, measles, menstrual cramps, rheumatic pains, and tiredness. Goatweed tea is especially popular in the Bahamas and from Belize south to Venezuela, where it is consumed as a substitute for black tea. The name goatweed relates to goats eating the plants when other barnyard animals ignore them.
**Uses:** The typical use is to pick fresh leaves, wash them, and let them dry until brown. Crush the dried leaves and boil them as you would any tea. Sweeten to taste with sugar or honey.

# SIMAROUBACEAE (QUASSIA FAMILY)

## PARADISE TREE
*Simarouba glauca*

**Also called:** Bitterwood
**Nativity:** Native
**Florida range:** Brevard and Collier Counties south through the coastal counties into the Florida Keys
**Habitat:** Hardwood hammocks
**Description:** Dioecious tree, up to 40' tall, with alternate, compound leaves bearing 10–20 narrowly oblong, glossy leaflets averaging 1½"–2" long and ¾"–1¼" wide. Small flowers are in long, open panicles, and female trees produce oblong-oval, ¾" fruits that ripen from green to red to purplish black. Fruits are present in late spring and early summer.
**Cautions:** Unripe fruits are very astringent. In supplement form, it is unsafe for women who are breast-feeding, and it is mentioned in the literature as an abortifacient, so women in early stages of pregnancy should avoid taking Simarouba supplements. Eating paradise tree fruits in quantity may lead to constipation.
**Comments:** The fruits of paradise tree have been medically proven to have important medicinal properties to aid in battling cancer and to help alleviate the effects of chemotherapy. Medical researchers have also found antibiotic values that can cure bacterial, protozoan, and viral diseases without any negative side effects. The leaves and bark have a long history of medicinal uses to treat malaria and dysentery.
**Uses:** Fully ripe fruits from female trees can be picked and eaten, but will be slightly astringent even when ripe. The seeds are harvested in tropical American countries to produce a cooking oil that is free of bad cholesterol.

# SMILACACEAE (GREENBRIER FAMILY)

Earleaf greenbrier shoots

## EARLEAF GREENBRIER
*Smilax auriculata*

**Also called:** Wild-bamboo

**Nativity:** Native

**Florida range:** Throughout the Florida mainland

**Habitat:** Pinelands, hammock margins, coastal strand

**Description:** Spiny, high-climbing, tendriled vine with narrowly ovate to ovate-elliptic leaves that typically have earlike lobes at the base, often with silvery-white mottling. Clusters of small, fragrant, green flowers produce round, hard, black to purplish-maroon seeds.

**Cautions:** Sharp spines may be present on the stems, but are always present at the base of the plant.

**Comments:** There are 11 other *Smilax* species in Florida, but not all of them produce spines on the stems. This species is absent from the Florida Keys but is replaced by the wickedly spiny *Smilax bona-nox* and *Smilax havanensis.* The tender new growth of these two can be eaten in the same manner as this species.

**Uses:** The tender young shoots, or growing tips, can be picked and eaten raw, and taste similar to asparagus. It is mentioned in the literature that foragers should only eat the shoots raw in small quantities, but without explanation, although it may be due to tannins. The shoots of some species are bitter, so nibble first. The tender young shoots can also be steamed or boiled and served as a side dish. The plant produces masses of underground, potato-like tubers that can be dug up, washed, and boiled as a starchy vegetable. The rhizomes of sarsparilla vine (*Smilax pumila*) of the southeastern states, including Florida, are used to flavor root beer.

# SOLANACEAE (NIGHTSHADE FAMILY)

## BIRD PEPPER
*Capsicum annuum* var. *glabriusculum*

**Also called:** Pequin, chiltepin

**Nativity:** Native

**Florida range:** Wakulla, Levy, Alachua, and Flagler Counties discontinuously south into the Florida Keys; much more common in the southern counties

**Habitat:** Hammock margins, edges of mangroves, and along trails bisecting those habitats

**Description:** This small shrub can reach about 6' tall with alternate, ovate-lanceolate leaves averaging 1"–1½" long and ⅜"–¾" wide. The white, 5-lobed flowers average about ⅜" wide and produce ellipsoid fruits to about ⅜" long, ripening from green to red.

**Cautions:** Juice from the peppers can cause very painful irritation to the eyes. The heat scale of the bird pepper is ranked at 90,000 Scoville units, making it up to ten times hotter than a jalapeño, so be very careful about wiping your eyes after handling ripe fruits.

**Comments:** Like its name implies, birds feast on the small peppers, especially mockingbirds, but they gulp them down whole and do not experience any of the heat. There are a few select Florida native-plant nurseries that sell bird pepper plants. Give the plants a sunny or semi-shady spot, and hope you get to harvest the peppers before the mockingbirds find them. In Mexico they are highly revered and command a much higher price in marketplaces than other hot peppers. I once entered a chili cookoff contest and added lots of bird peppers to cubed sirloin, tomato sauce, water, and spices (no beans). A newspaper reporter asked what I thought made my chili stand out above the other entries, and I told her that it helps improve your memory. When she asked how that is possible, I explained that, after enjoying a bowl of it, the next time you go to the bathroom you'll remember you ate it! But, even at 90,000 Scoville units, bird peppers pale in comparison to the Carolina reaper and Trinidad scorpion pepper, each ranking well above 1 million Scoville units in the heat scale.

**Uses:** Bird peppers can be eaten fresh if you like extreme heat. If the heat is too much to bear, drinking cold milk will help alleviate your suffering much better than water. Bird peppers can be added to chili, spaghetti sauce, and other dishes during cooking, but I would suggest first dicing them up and adding only about three or four of them to see if you like that amount of heat. Add fewer, or more, the next time. Removing the seeds before cooking slightly lowers the heat index. As my dear botanist friend Dan Austin (1943–2015) once wrote, "The next time you bite into a chili-laced dish, and the tears start running down your cheeks, remember that you are eating healthy food."

## TABASCO PEPPER
*Capsicum frutescens*

**Also called:** Pimiento, cayenne pepper, red pepper
**Nativity:** Native
**Florida range:** Vouchered from Citrus and Volusia Counties in north-central Florida south into the Florida Keys but mostly in the counties below Lake Okeechobee
**Habitat:** Sandy and rocky soils in open, sunny habitats, including disturbed sites
**Description:** Multi-branched, shrubby species, often with zigzagging stems, reaching 3'–6' tall with lanceolate to ovate leaves averaging 1"–3" long and ½"–1" wide. The 5-lobed, white to greenish-white flowers produce erect peppers that ripen red, each measuring up to 1½" long.
**Cautions:** Juice from the peppers can cause very painful irritation to the eyes, so be careful not to wipe your eyes with your hands after handling the peppers.
**Comments:** The tabasco pepper ranks between 30,000 and 50,000 Scoville units on the heat scale, making it 3 to 6 times hotter than a jalapeño. It was named after the Mexican state

of Tabasco and is best known for its use to make tabasco sauce for cooking and as a condiment. It is regarded as the most-consumed hot pepper in the world.

**Uses:** Use them as you would any hot pepper to spice up sauces, stews, or other dishes. You can also make tabasco jelly!

## RECIPE

### Spicy Peach Jelly

3–5 seeded tabasco peppers, chopped
1½ cups chopped, peeled fresh or frozen peaches (some recipes use strawberries)
1 tablespoon lime juice
1 cup white vinegar
2½ cups chopped bell peppers
1½ (1.75-ounce) packets of Sure-Jell
5 cups granulated sugar (white or turbinado)
7 sterilized 8-ounce canning jars

1. Add seeded and chopped tabasco peppers, peaches, lime juice, and vinegar to a blender and blend briefly on medium speed until ingredients are well combined.

2. Pour blender contents into a medium to large stainless-steel pot, add the chopped bell peppers, and place on a stove burner set on high while adding the Sure-Jell a teaspoon at a time, stirring until it is completely mixed.

3. Stir in the sugar and, when the mixture comes to a boil, stir continuously for about 3 minutes. Remove from heat.

4. Spoon into canning jars and seal. Fill a large pot with water and bring to a boil, then boil the sealed jars for 10 minutes. Let jars cool overnight.

*Note:* This jelly will not set up like commercial jelly, so it's best to refrigerate a jar before opening for use. Store the other jars in a cool, dry place or give to friends.

# WALTER'S GROUNDCHERRY
*Physalis walteri*

**Also called:** Husk tomato, ground cherry
**Nativity:** Native
**Florida range:** Common throughout peninsular Florida into the Florida Keys, but discontinuous through the Panhandle
**Habitat:** Pinelands, forest margins, canopy gaps, coastal dunes, and disturbed sites
**Description:** Herbaceous perennial from 12"–24" tall with erect or spreading pubescent branches and moderate to densely pubescent, elliptic or ovate to ovate-lanceolate leaf blades, each measuring 1½"–4" long and ½"–2" wide. Pendent, ¾"–1", solitary flowers are axillary. The flowers are yellow with brown markings in the throat. Globose fruits reach about ½" wide, ripening yellow, and are hidden inside a green, lantern-like husk that turns light tan with age.
**Cautions:** Dr. Julia Morton (1912–1996) noted that the leaves and green, unripe fruits of *Physalis* species are somewhat toxic due to the presence of solanines, which can have a laxative effect and cause the kidneys to produce more urine.
**Comments:** There are 9 members of this genus in Florida, and all are native and have edible fruits. Two common edible species found in tropical American marketplaces and in Hispanic groceries in Florida are the tomatillo (*Physalis ixocarpa*) and the ground cherry (*Physalis pruinosa*), neither of which are native to Florida.
**Uses:** Ripe, yellow fruits from species in this genus can be picked and eaten fresh, cooked, or added to salads, soups, stews, chili rellenos, or tacos. They can also be used to make salsa, guacamole, preserves, and dessert toppings. Uses are similar to how you might use tomatoes.

## EVERGLADES TOMATO
*Solanum lycopersicum (*formerly *Lycopersicon esculentum)*

**Also called:** Garden tomato
**Nativity:** Introduced from South America
**Florida range:** Scattered local populations throughout Florida
**Habitat:** Disturbed sites, including residential landscapes, roadsides, vacant lots, and trail margins
**Description:** Herbaceous annual or short-lived perennial with vine-like, pubescent branches and compound leaves bearing 5–9 toothed leaflets. Yellow, 5-lobed flowers are produced on branched, axillary stems and measure about ½" wide. Globose fruits range in size from ⅝" to about 4" wide, ripening red or sometimes yellow, depending on the cultivar. There are numerous cultivars in the nursery trade.
**Cautions:** Some members of the genus *Solanum* are toxic.
**Comments:** "Everglades tomato" is a local name because this wild tomato is known to sprout in the Everglades region after hurricanes disturb the soil, which also happens in residential areas. After Hurricane Wilma in 2005, it sprouted all over our 1-acre property near Homestead and is still persisting from seeds 17 years later, not that I'm complaining. One issue is whether this cherry-type wild tomato represents *Solanum lycopersicum* or if it actually is *Solanum pimpinellifolium*, which it closely resembles. Regardless, the tiny tomatoes it produces are quite tasty and would be a welcomed treat for foragers who happen upon

fruiting plants in their travels. Even though it is a non-native naturalized species in Florida, it is not creating any adverse environmental issues.

**Uses:** Use them as you would any cherry tomato, either picked and eaten fresh or added to salads and spaghetti sauce—or make some tomato soup.

---

RECIPE

**Everglades Tomato Soup**

2 pounds Everglades tomatoes
4 tablespoons plant-based butter (or unsalted regular butter)
1 medium onion, chopped
1½ cups water (or vegetable broth)
½ teaspoon salt

1. Add tomatoes to a large stainless-steel pot, cover with water, and boil for 15 minutes. Remove from heat, pour off the water, and mash the tomatoes with a potato masher.

2. Melt the butter over medium heat in a large stainless-steel pan, then add the onion, water, tomato mash, and salt. Bring to a simmer and cook uncovered for 30–40 minutes, stirring occasionally.

3. Using a blender, blend the mixture in batches (it is wise to remove the center insert in the lid and cover it with a kitchen towel so the hot soup will not make the lid pop off).

4. When finished, the soup can be served immediately or poured into mason jars and refrigerated.

# TALINACEAE (TALINUM FAMILY)

## VERDOLAGA-FRANCESA
*Talinum fruticosum* (formerly *Talinum triangulare*)

**Also called:** Ceylon spinach, French purslane, Surinam purslane, waterleaf

**Nativity:** Introduced from tropical America and the West Indies

**Florida range:** Vouchered in Pinellas, Polk, Lee, Miami-Dade, and the Monroe County Keys

**Habitat:** Open, disturbed sites

**Description:** Herbaceous perennial typically reaching about 36"–48" tall with obovate to oblanceolate, fleshy leaves that average 1"–2" long and ½"–¾" wide. Pink flowers are about ¾" across and are produced all year.

**Cautions:** The leaves are high in oxalates, so they should only be eaten sparingly (if at all) by those who are susceptible to kidney stones, but this is also true for spinach, kale, collard greens, and other popular leaf vegetables in marketplaces.

**Comments:** The common name translates from Spanish to "French purslane." This species is not widely cultivated in Florida, but it is sparingly naturalized in central and southern Florida, especially in the Florida Keys. It is used medicinally as a diuretic, which helps remove sodium through your urine and helps lower blood pressure. Other medicinal uses are for treating gastrointestinal disorders, scabies (caused by mites), and anemia (low red blood cell count).

**Uses:** The leaves and flowers can be picked and eaten fresh, or the leaves can be steamed or boiled in the same manner as you would spinach. The plant is widely consumed in tropical regions worldwide as a nutritious potherb, especially in Africa.

# TYPHACEAE (CATTAIL FAMILY)

## CATTAIL
*Typha* spp.

**Also called:** Bulrush (Great Britain), punks (Australia), raupo (New Zealand)

**Nativity:** Native

**Florida range:** Two species occur in Florida, and one or the other can be found throughout Florida (*Typha domingensis* is pictured).

**Habitat:** Freshwater wetlands, including swamps, sloughs, ponds, lakes, ditches, canals, wet depressions, and edges of streams and rivers

**Description:** Clump-forming herbaceous species with long, linear leaves 6'–10' tall or more and about ¾"–1" wide. Male flowers produce large amounts of pollen and are borne above the long, brown, cylindrical clusters of female flowers on the same spike. Seeds are wind dispersed.

**Cautions:** Cattails are found in the same habitat as American alligators and cottonmouth moccasins, so use due caution. Ensure that you are harvesting from a clean water source and not adjacent to agricultural fields where there could be pesticide runoff, or canals next to industrial plants that could be a source of pollution.

**Comments:** Cattails should be familiar to everyone because they are ubiquitous in freshwater habitats and often seen along roadways that bisect their habitat. Three species occur in the United States and 2 of those are widespread in Florida. There are also 2 hybrids between these species, but no hybrids have been reported in Florida even though the Florida native species grow in mixed colonies and most likely hybridize. The exponential spread of cattails in the Everglades region has been linked to high levels of phosphates from fertilizers, both from the sugarcane industry below Lake Okeechobee and from residential development to the north of Lake Okeechobee.

**Uses:** Cattails are more useful as food than most plants, and all parts are edible in at least one stage of their growth. The pollen can be harvested and used as an additive in flour for baked or fried foods and is extremely high in Vitamin C. Tiny male flowers are produced on the flowering spike above the female flowers and produce an abundance of pollen that can be shaken into a large jar or bag, or pulled off with your fingers prior to maturity when it blows off into the wind. The very young flowering stems can be broken off, peeled like an ear of corn, and then eaten either raw or boiled, having a flavor somewhat similar to corn. The thick rhizomes can be harvested, trimmed of their side shoots, and then baked, grilled, or boiled. The leaves can be pulled off, and the white, tender base is edible raw.

# VERBENACEAE (VERBENA FAMILY)

## FIDDLEWOOD
*Citharexylum spinosum* (formerly *Citharexylum fruticosum*)

**Also called:** Faithful wood (translated from *bois fidéle* in French)
**Nativity:** Native
**Florida range:** Coastal counties from Sarasota and Brevard Counties south along both coasts into the Florida Keys
**Habitat:** Hammocks, or occasionally as an invader in pinelands where it is either killed or kept shrubby by fire
**Description:** Dioecious tree to 18' tall or more with glossy, opposite, oblanceolate leaves averaging 3"–4" long and 1½"–2" wide with orange petioles. Seedling leaves have spiny margins (hence the species name *spinosum*), but mature leaves have smooth margins. Very fragrant, ⅜" flowers are on pendent spikes. Fruits are globose, to about ⅜" wide, ripening from orange to purplish black.
**Cautions:** If you grow fiddlewood as a landscape tree, be advised that it might be defoliated annually by tent caterpillars, but the caterpillars attract hungry birds.

**Comments:** Although the fruits are described as being edible, Dr. Julia Morton (1912–1996) wrote that "the fruit is edible but not good," and Dr. Dan Austin (1943–2015) opined that their edibility "might depend on how hungry you may be." Having tasted them myself, I conclude that both are correct. There are numerous bush medicine uses for the bark, leaf tea, and fruits, including treating pain from exposure to chilly wind, as a treatment for sores on a child's body, and to alleviate indigestion. The most useful part of the tree is its hard wood, which is used for fenceposts, cabinetry, boat-building, and in the manufacture of fiddles and other musical instruments.

**Uses:** The ripe fruits can be picked and eaten fresh, and then you can determine for yourself if they are good enough to go back for seconds. In other words, they are edible but not particularly eatable.

# VIBURNACEAE (VIBURNUM FAMILY)

## COMMON ELDERBERRY
### *Sambucus canadensis*

**Also called:** American elder, common elder
**Nativity:** Native
**Florida range:** Throughout all of mainland Florida (absent from the Florida Keys)
**Habitat:** Wet ground, including freshwater swamps, mesic forests, floodplains, ditches, and shorelines of lakes, ponds, streams, rivers, and springs
**Description:** Small tree to 12' tall or more with opposite, pinnately compound leaves bearing 5–9 narrowly lanceolate, toothed leaflets, each measuring about 2"–4" long and ½"–1" wide. White flowers, each with 5 rounded petals, are in dense corymbs that average 5"–8" across and stand above the leaves. Oval, dark purple to black, ¼" fruits are in drooping clusters.
**Cautions:** Leaves, stems, roots, seeds, and unripe fruits are toxic and can be lethal if eaten in very high doses. There is a 1983 incident in California where a religious group took quantities of ripe elderberries along with leaves and young stems and made juice with a stainless-steel press. It was consumed the following day, and 8 people became nauseous and experienced

## RECIPE

**Wild Elderberry Syrup**

1 cup fully ripe elderberries (if fresh elderberries are not available, dried elderberries can be found in markets or ordered online)
4 cups water
5 whole cloves
1 tablespoon freshly grated ginger (or 1 teaspoon dried ginger)
1 cup honey

1. In a large, stainless-steel pot, add elderberries, water, cloves, and ginger and bring to a boil. Reduce heat and simmer until thickened (45–60 minutes). Remove from heat and allow mixture to cool.

2. Pour mixture through a fine-mesh strainer into a large bowl, mashing the berries with the back of a wooden spoon to remove the seeds and collect as much liquid as possible.

3. Add the honey and stir (heating the honey first will make it dissolve quicker).

4. Pour into mason jars and refrigerate. Delicious on pancakes or waffles.

## RECIPE

**Wild Elderberry Cordial**
(non-alcoholic)

2½ cups fresh, ripe elderberries
Shaved rind from ½ lemon
2½ cups water
1 cup granulated sugar (turbinado sugar is best)
1 tablespoon lemon juice

1. Wash the berries in a colander and pour them into a large stainless-steel pot. Add the lemon rind and water. Simmer on low heat for 30 minutes and skim off any foam.

2. Pour mixture through a fine-mesh strainer or a colander lined with muslin cloth into a bowl, pressing the berries with a wooden spoon to remove the seeds and collect as much juice as possible.

3. Add the sugar and lemon juice. Stir until the sugar is dissolved. Try a sample and add more sugar or lemon to suit your taste.

4. Pour into a sterilized bottle (empty liquor bottles work well). Serve in shot glasses.

acute gastrointestinal and neurological symptoms. They were flown by helicopter to a local hospital where all recovered. The deadly poisonous spotted water hemlock (*Cicuta maculata*) shares the same habitat with elderberry and has similar-looking flowers arranged in an umbel, but with a notch on the tip of the petals that is not present on elderberry. See the Poisonous Plants chapter in this guide.

**Comments:** Elderberry ranges across much of the United States into Canada and is one of the most well-known edible plants among foragers.

**Uses:** The flowers can be boiled to make a pleasant hot or cold tea, or the entire flower cluster can be dipped in batter and fried. The fully ripe fruits can be eaten fresh in moderation or strained to remove the seeds and used to make pies, syrups, cordials, jams, ketchup, or wine. Look for recipes on the internet or try the three included here.

---

RECIPE

### Elderberry Ketchup

This recipe is modified from a book published in 1888, titled *Family Living on $500 a Year: A Daily Reference Book for Young and Inexperienced Housewives*, by Juliet Corson.

3 cups ripe elderberries
About 1 cup water
⅓ cup white vinegar
¼ cup granulated sugar
½ teaspoon allspice
½ teaspoon cinnamon
½ teaspoon ground cloves
½ teaspoon pepper
½ teaspoon salt

1. Wash elderberries in a colander, then add them to a stainless-steel pot with the water. Cook the elderberries gently until you can squash them through a sieve with a wooden spoon to separate the seeds and skin from the pulp.

2. Discard the skin and seeds, return the pulp to the pot, and adding the remaining ingredients. Bring to a low boil while stirring until it thickens to the consistency of ketchup.

***Note:*** Double or triple this recipe if you have enough elderberries. You can also use native grapes, or combine grapes with elderberries.

---

# VITACEAE (GRAPE FAMILY)

## MUSCADINE GRAPE
*Vitis rotundifolia*

**Also called:** Wild grape

**Nativity:** Native

**Florida range:** Throughout all of Florida

**Habitat:** Edges of forests, pinelands, canopy gaps, fencerows, and disturbed sites

**Description:** High-climbing, sparsely branched, woody vine with unbranched tendrils. The coarsely toothed leaves are rounded in outline and average 2"–4" wide with a glabrous upper and lower surface. Flowers are unisexual and are formed in clusters. The round berries ripen dark purple or black and average ⅜" wide, but may be larger.

**Cautions:** Unripe grapes will be tart and may cause diarrhea.

**Comments:** Grapes are well-known to everyone worldwide, but it is probably safe to say that most Floridians have never tasted the fruits of wild grapes. Although Florida is home to 6 native species of grapes, *Vitis rotundifolia* is the most common and widespread species in the state, being found in every county from the far western Panhandle south through the Florida Keys. Another very common species, summer grape (*Vitis aestivalis*), is found nearly statewide, but is absent from the Florida Keys. All produce edible fruits. Dr. Dan Austin (1943–2015), in his fabulous book, *Florida Ethnobotany*, wrote, "Use of the fruit of *Vitis* is older than the history of any culture." This says quite a lot, knowing how long some cultures have been in existence, and that grapes were being used as food, medicines, and beverages longer than any culture existed. Wild grapes are easy to identify, with most of them bearing rounded, coarsely toothed leaves, but identifying them to species is a bit more challenging. Key features to look for are whether the tendrils are branched, unbranched, or absent, and whether the leaves are smooth or pubescent, plus the color of the pubescence on the undersides of the leaves. Fox grape or frost grape (*Vitis vulpine*) of northern and central Florida often has deeply 5-lobed leaves with paler undersides.

**Uses:** The slightly tart ripe grapes can be picked and eaten fresh and have been an important food source for both native cultures and settlers throughout North America. The fruits can be used for juice, syrups, jellies, and jams, added to fruit salads, and used to make wine. To flavor gin, white rum, or vodka, simply add a half cup of ripe fruits to a pint of liquor and let it sit for about 6 months. The young new leaves and stems can be steamed and eaten as greens or wrapped around other foods before baking. The ripe fruits can also be dried, like raisins, but they are seedy.

## RECIPE

**Wild Grape Jelly**

4 cups ripe wild grapes, washed
¼ cup water
Granulated sugar

1. Mash the grapes in a large bowl with the back of a wooden spoon, or use low speed in a blender.

2. Add the grape mash and water to a stainless-steel pot and cook over medium heat for 15 minutes.

3. Pour the mixture through a strainer into a glass bowl and discard the skin and seeds. Allow to sit overnight, then pour the juice into a 2-cup measuring glass to see how much juice remains.

4. Add the juice and an equal amount of granulated sugar into a stainless-steel pan and boil until thickened.

5. Either refrigerate in containers or spoon into sterilized canning jars, seal, and place each jar in boiling water for 10 minutes, then cool and store.

# XIMENIACEAE (XIMENIA FAMILY)

## HOG PLUM
*Ximenia americana*

**Also called:** Tallowwood, purge-nut
**Nativity:** Native
**Florida range:** From the northern peninsula south through the Florida Keys
**Habitat:** Hammock margins, wooded swamps, and sandhills
**Description:** Thorny, hemiparasitic tree typically 10'–16' tall but may be taller. Leaves range from elliptic, lanceolate, ovate, or obovate and average 1"–1¾" long and ½"–1" wide. Very fragrant, white to pale yellow, hairy flowers are clustered in the leaf axils. The oblong fruits ripen yellow and average about 1" long and ¾" wide.
**Cautions:** The branches are armed with sharp thorns. Unripe fruits are astringent, and the seeds are not only a powerful laxative, but they also contain small traces of cyanide.
**Comments:** This tree photosynthesizes like normal trees, but it also derives nutrients by parasitizing the roots of other trees. It is most commonly found along the edges of hardwood forests and along elevated trails or roads that cut through mixed hardwood swamps.
**Uses:** The tasty, fully ripe fruits can be picked and eaten, but avoid eating the seeds (see Cautions). Carib Indians boiled the tender new leaves as a vegetable. The fruits are made into a syrup in Panama and the West Indies, or fermented and made into a form of beer. The bark is astringent and has been boiled, cooled, and used as a bath to cure skin diseases. Dr. Dan Austin (1943–2015) noted that the roots are chewed in Panama to alleviate toothache and to treat vomiting, sleeping sickness, fevers, venereal disease, and ringworm.

# XYRIDACEAE (YELLOWEYED GRASS FAMILY)

*Xyris elliottii*                                    *Xyris caroliniana*

## YELLOWEYED GRASS
*Xyris* spp.

**Nativity:** Native

**Florida range:** Varies by species: *Xyris caroliniana* is found statewide, including the Florida Keys, and *Xyris elliottii* is found statewide but absent in the Florida Keys (both pictured here)

**Habitat:** Varies by species but mostly sandy flatwoods, sandy shorelines, pinelands, bogs, and prairies

**Description:** Perennial herb with simple, erect stems. Leaves are alternate, 2-ranked, with linear leaf blades. Flowers are solitary in bract axils with 3 prominent sepals.

**Cautions:** *Xyris isoetifolia*, *Xyris longisepala*, and *Xyris panacea* are state-listed endangered species, and *Xyris scabrifolia* is a state-listed threatened species. These species should not be harvested due to their protected status.

**Comments:** There are 25 *Xyris* species native to Florida and they require a working knowledge of a botanical key to correctly identify them. Some are found statewide, while others have limited ranges, with one endemic species, *Xyris correlliorum*, that is known only from Highlands County and should be listed as federal- and state-endangered.

**Uses:** An infusion was made from the roots of various species by Native Americans in the Southeast and used to treat diarrhea, skin problems, colds, and pulmonary disorders. Infusions are made simply by placing 2 or 3 tablespoons of dried herbs, roots, or flowers into a tea strainer placed in a cup. Boil water in a pan and pour the hot water into the cup, then cover. Allow to steep for up to 1 hour and strain.

# GLOSSARY

**Abortifacient:** Plants that may induce miscarriage as well as causing health risks to the mother.

**Annual:** Completing its life cycle from seed to maturity and death in one year.

**Anthesis:** Flowering period.

**Cladode:** The pads of a cactus.

**Compound leaf:** A leaf divided into two or more leaflets.

**Corymb:** A flower cluster with the outer flowers on longer pedicels than the inner flowers.

**Crenulate:** Scalloped.

**Cultivar:** Abbreviation of cultivated variety.

**Deciduous:** Becoming leafless during winter.

**Decoction:** A medicinal preparation made from a plant by concentrating the essence of the leaves or roots by boiling.

**Dioecious:** Male and female flowers produced on separate plants.

**Drupe:** A one-seeded fruit.

**Ellipsoid/elliptical:** Twice as long as wide.

**Globose:** Having a spherical, or oval, shape.

**Hemiparasite, hemiparasitic:** A plant that parasitizes the roots of other plants but also photosynthesizes.

**Herbaceous:** Not woody.

**Hilum:** A scar on a seed marking the point of attachment.

**Inflorescence:** A group or cluster of flowers on a stem.

**Infusion:** A drink prepared from the leaves of a plant or herb.

**Introduced:** Purposely or inadvertently imported from another country or region; not native.

**Invasive:** A species that escapes cultivation and invades native habitats, often negatively altering their function by spreading aggressively and crowding out native species.

**Lanceolate:** Lance-shaped; pointed on both ends.

**Naturalized:** Growing and reproducing outside of cultivation in disturbed sites or natural areas; not native.

**Oblanceolate:** Lanceolate with the narrower end toward the base.

**Obovate:** Ovate with the narrower end toward the base.

**Obovoid:** Ovoid with the narrower end toward the base.

**Ovate/Ovoid:** Egg-shaped in outline.

**Pedicel:** The stalk of a flower in an inflorescence or the stalk of a fruit.

**Perennial:** Living three or more years.

**Serrulate:** Bearing small, fine teeth along the margin.

**Umbel:** A flower cluster with flowers on short pedicels attached to a common center, forming a flat or curved arrangement.

**Vouchered:** A plant or plant part that has been collected, pressed, labeled with collection data, and deposited in an herbarium to officially document its presence in the location where it was collected.

# REFERENCES

Allen, Cheyenne. *Native American Herbalist's Bible.* 2021. Perfect Bound 2.0 Design and Writing.

Atlas of Florida Plants, Institute for Systematic Botany, https://florida.plant atlas.usf.edu/

Austin, Daniel F. *Florida Ethnobotany.* 2004. CRC Press, Boca Raton, FL.

Corson, Juliet. *Family Living on $500 a Year: A Daily Reference Book for Young and Inexperienced Housewives.* 1888. Harper & Brothers, Franklin Square, NY.

*Flora of North America*, https://floranorthamerica.org

Hammer, Roger L. *Central Florida Wildflowers.* 2016. Rowman & Littlefield, Guilford, CT.

Hammer, Roger L. *Complete Guide to Florida Wildflowers.* 2018. Rowman & Littlefield, Guilford, CT.

Hammer, Roger L. *Everglades Wildflowers.* Second edition, 2014. Rowman & Littlefield, Guilford, CT.

Hammer, Roger L. *Wildflowers of the Florida Keys.* Second edition, 2022. Rowman & Littlefield, Guilford, CT.

Honychurch, Penelope N. *Caribbean Wild Plants & Their Uses.* Second edition, 1991. Macmillan Education Ltd., London, England.

Kimbrough, James. *Common Florida Mushrooms.* 2000. University of Florida Institute of Food and Agricultural Sciences, Gainesville, FL.

Lantz, Peggy. *Florida's Edible Wild Plants: A Guide to Collecting and Cooking.* 2014. University Press of Florida, Gainesville, FL.

McCormack, Jeffrey Holt, Kathleen Maier, and Patricia B. Wallens. *Bush Medicine of the Bahamas.* 2011. JHM Designs Publications, Charlottesville, VA.

Moerman, Daniel E. *Native American Ethnobotany.* 1998. Timber Press, Portland, OR.

Morton, Julia F. *Folk Remedies of the Low Country.* 1974. E.A. Seemann, Miami, FL.

Morton, Julia F. *Plants Poisonous to People in Florida and Other Warm Areas.* 1982. Southeastern Printing Co., Inc., Stuart, FL.

Morton, Julia F. *Wild Plants for Survival in South Florida.* Second edition, 1968. Hurricane House Publishers, Inc., Miami, FL.

Saunders, Charles Francis. *Edible and Useful Wild Plants of the United States and Canada.* Third edition, 1948. Dover Publications, Inc., New York, NY.

Weakley, Alan S., et al. *Flora of the Southeastern United States.* 2022. Chapel Hill: University of North Carolina at Chapel Hill.

Yanovsky, E. *Food Plants of the North American Indians.* 1936. US Department of Agriculture, Washington, D.C.

# INDEX

# ABOUT THE AUTHOR

**Roger L. Hammer** is a professional naturalist and survivalist instructor for the Discovery Channel's reality TV show *Naked and Afraid*. He grew up in Cocoa Beach and served in the US Army from 1965 to 1968 as a tank gunner, ship winch operator, education specialist, and army recruiter. He was the manager of the 120-acre Castellow Hammock Nature Center for the Miami-Dade County Parks Department from 1977 to 2010. He received the first Marjory Stoneman Douglas Award presented by the Dade Chapter of the Florida Native Plant Society in 1982; Tropical Audubon Society honored him with the prestigious Charles Brookfield Medal in 1996; and in 2003 he received the Green Palmetto Award in Education from the Florida Native Plant Society. He has given keynote speeches at Florida Native Plant Society state conferences, the 2008 World Orchid Conference, and the 2016 Florida Wildflower Foundation symposium. He was also the opening speaker at the American Orchid Society's one-hundred-year anniversary celebration held in Miami's historic Biltmore Hotel in 2022. In 2012 he received an honorary Doctor of Science degree from Florida International University. He is the author of *Everglades Wildflowers*, *Central Florida Wildflowers*, *Wildflowers of the Florida Keys*, *Complete Guide to Florida Wildflowers*, *Exploring Everglades National Park and the Surrounding Area*, *Paddling Everglades and Biscayne National Parks*, *Florida Icons: 50 Classic Views of the Sunshine State*, and *Attracting Hummingbirds and Butterflies in Tropical Florida*. He lives in Homestead with his wife, Michelle.